Managing
Information
Resources

Managing Information Resources

James Gatza, D.B.A., CPCU, AIM
Vice President and Director of Executive Education (deceased)
American Institute for CPCU

Alan J. Turner, CPCU
Assistant Vice President and Director of Information Systems
Financial Indemnity Co.

Norbert R. Stone, CPCU, CLU, ARe
President
Stone Associates

First Edition • 1995

American Institute for CPCU
720 Providence Road, Malvern, Pennsylvania 19355-0770

© 1995
American Institute for CPCU
All rights reserved. This book or any part thereof may not be reproduced without the written permission of the publisher.

First Edition • July 1995

Library of Congress Catalog Number 95-78604
International Standard Book Number 0-89463-070-9

Printed in the United States of America

Dedication

This text is dedicated to the memory of one of its authors, the late Dr. James Gatza, CPCU, AIM, vice president of the American Institute for CPCU and the Insurance Institute of America.

When asked how he was doing, Jim would invariably respond, with a grin, "I think I'll make it." Unfortunately, Jim died suddenly of a heart attack on February 2, 1995, at the age of 61. At the time of his death, he had compiled the manuscript for this book, but it had not yet been published.

During the past twenty-five years, Jim was responsible for the Management course of the CPCU curriculum as well as other aspects of management and supervisory education at the American Institute for CPCU and the Insurance Institute of America (IIA). He coauthored two other texts, *Decision Making in Administration* and *Managing Automated Activities*.

A native of Buffalo, NY, Jim received his bachelor's and master's degrees from the State University of New York at Buffalo. After serving five years as an electronic warfare officer in the United States Air Force, Jim received his doctoral degree from Harvard Business School in 1965. Jim spent five years on the faculty of Villanova University, including three years as chairman of the Department of Management, before joining the American Institute for CPCU and the Insurance Institute of America. For many years, he directed the IIA Associate in Management program and the IIA Program in Supervisory Management. As program director, he developed the Associate in Automation Management program and remained responsible for it until the time of his death. Jim also directed the Institutes' Advanced Executive Education program, co-sponsored by the Wharton School of the University of Pennsylvania. He had a number of Institute-wide marketing responsibilities and served as a frequent speaker at insurance industry meetings.

Jim's work over the past twenty-five years has had a profound influence on the management development of many thousands of insurance professionals, ranging from the novice to the chief executive. Jim's students, in turn, will go on to influence others for decades to come. But despite Jim's academic strengths, his friends and colleagues remember Jim's other interests. He and his wife, Kathleen, loved to travel. He was a student of art and architecture. He had a strong interest in jazz and was an avid collector of jazz recordings. He enjoyed volleyball several times a week and played his last game just two days before his death. In addition to his wife, Kathleen, Jim is survived by five children, four grandchildren, and a brother.

Foreword

The American Institute for Chartered Property Casualty Underwriters and the Insurance Institute of America are independent, nonprofit, educational organizations serving the needs of the property and liability insurance business. The Institutes develop a wide range of programs—curricula, study materials, and examinations—in response to the educational requirements of various elements of the business.

The American Institute confers the Chartered Property Casualty Underwriter (CPCU®) professional designation on those who meet the Institute's experience, ethics, and examination requirements.

The Insurance Institute of America offers associate designations and certificate programs in the following technical and managerial disciplines:

Accredited Adviser in Insurance (AAI®)
Associate in Claims (AIC)
Associate in Underwriting (AU)
Associate in Risk Management (ARM)
Associate in Loss Control Management (ALCM®)
Associate in Premium Auditing (APA®)
Associate in Management (AIM)
Associate in Research and Planning (ARP®)
Associate in Insurance Accounting and Finance (AIAF)
Associate in Automation Management (AAM®)
Associate in Marine Insurance Management (AMIM®)
Associate in Reinsurance (ARe)
Associate in Fidelity and Surety Bonding (AFSB)
Associate in Insurance Services (AIS)
Certificate in General Insurance
Certificate in Insurance Regulation

Certificate in Supervisory Management
Certificate in Introduction to Underwriting
Certificate in Introduction to Claims
Certificate in Introduction to Property and Liability Insurance
Certificate in Business Writing

The Institutes began publishing textbooks in 1976 to help students meet the national examination standards. Since that time, we have produced more than eighty individual textbook volumes. Despite the vast differences in the subjects and purposes of these volumes, they all have much in common. First, each book is specifically designed to increase knowledge and develop skills that can improve job performance and help students achieve the educational objectives of the course for which it is assigned. Second, all of the manuscripts of our texts are widely reviewed before publication, by both insurance business practitioners and members of the academic community. In addition, all of our texts and course guides reflect the work of Institute staff members. These writing or editing duties are seen as an integral part of their professional responsibilities, and no one earns a royalty based on the sale of our texts. We have proceeded in this way to avoid even the appearance of any conflict of interests. Finally, the revisions of our texts often incorporate improvements suggested by students and course leaders.

We welcome criticisms of and suggestions for improving our publications. It is only with such constructive comments that we can hope to improve the quality of our study materials. Please direct any comments you may have on this text to the Curriculum Department of the Institutes.

Norman A. Baglini, Ph.D., CPCU, CLU
President and Chief Executive Officer

Preface

Managing Information Resources is a new book for CPCU 7, replacing *Computers in Insurance*. As indicated by its title, the book focuses on information resources rather than on computers. In insurance, information is a vital resource. Therefore, for those studying management within the CPCU program, understanding the concepts and technology involved in managing those resources is particularly important.

This book discusses how to integrate information resources with business needs, describes various information technologies, and explains how to manage automated activities. It forms three assignments within CPCU 7, which deals primarily with management within insurance organizations. For those seeking an in-depth understanding of how to manage automated resources, the Insurance Institute of America's Associate in Automation Management (AAM) program is recommended.

Part of the process of developing an Institute textbook includes having the book reviewed by experts in the book's content area. The work of such reviewers significantly improves the quality of the book. We appreciate the contributions of the following outside reviewers:

Frank J. Gray, CPCU
Royal Insurance

David Leitschuh, CPCU, AIC, ARM
Marsh & McLennan, Inc.

Martin O'Grady, CPCU
Allstate Insurance Company

Art Pavelle
Consultant

Thanks also go to Thomas E. Leicht, AIM, AAM, vice president, American Institute for CPCU, and to Peter L. Miller, director of information systems, American Institute for CPCU, who also reviewed the chapters of this book.

The technology that allows us to effectively manage information resources will continue to change and so must this book. We welcome your comments and suggestions, which you can send to:

> George A. White, CPCU, AIM
> Vice President
> American Institute for CPCU

Contents

1 Integrating Information Resources with Business Needs   1

The Changing Business Climate   2

Information Resources Objectives   10

Information Resources Evaluation   19

Summary   22

2 Information Technologies   25

Image Processing   25

Application Development Tools and Techniques   29

Hardware Platforms   32

Artificial Intelligence Applications   37

Groupware   40

Graphical User Interfaces   41

Database Technology   44

Information Retrieval   46

Voice and Speech Technologies   47

Electronic Data Interchange   48

Multimedia   51

Implementing New Technologies   52

Applications   54

Summary   57

3 Managing Automated Activities   59

Special Challenges in Managing Information Resources   59

Managing Automation Projects   67

Managing System Growth   79

Agency/Company Interface   83

Protecting Information Assets   89

Summary   95

Index   97

Chapter 1

Integrating Information Resources With Business Needs

Information is the paramount tool for doing insurance work. A computer or a computer terminal sits on virtually every desk in insurance organizations of all kinds: companies, agencies, brokerage firms, adjusting firms, and organizations providing specialized services to the insurance business. In one sense, automation of the insurance business might appear complete because insurance has been extensively automated for many years. In another sense, the process of automation continues as automation is required to solve new problems and perform additional tasks. In that second sense, the quest for better information and for better information systems will never end. Any organization—from small agency to global insurer—must manage its information resources to survive in an industry facing changes of unprecedented magnitude and speed.

This text explores the insurance organization's information resources and information resources management. The term **information resources** refers to the following:

- Information system of the organization
- Information resources consisting of the computer system (hardware, software, networks, and communication facilities)
- Information available from the system
- Skill of organization members in using the system and information

The organizations constituting the insurance business continuously seek to improve their information resources. For that reason, this text will seldom specify that an idea pertains only to insurers, agencies, brokerages, or other kinds of organizations. Instead, the term "insurance organization" will often be used, indicating that the idea being presented applies to many of the organizations within insurance.

This book's objective is to provide an understanding of insurance information resources and their management. If this objective is achieved, many readers will be able to use this understanding to improve their information resources. The authors assume that a few innocent bystanders simply observe and use insurance information. However, most people who work in insurance and related fields have the opportunity to control information.

Chapter 1 explores ways in which insurance organizations and their information resources are undergoing major changes. Chapter 2 examines the technologies that enhance information resources. Chapter 3 provides ideas to assist in managing information resources.

This chapter begins by examining the changing business climate. The chapter then examines the contemporary objectives influencing information resources development. Finally, it suggests criteria that should be used to evaluate the effectiveness of information resources.

The Changing Business Climate

The business world is experiencing unprecedented change. Among the forces that are reshaping business organizations are the following:

- Focus on customer satisfaction
- Emphasis on service
- Focus on core business
- Decline of command and control management
- Closer relationships with suppliers and customers
- Outsourcing products and services
- Business alignments
- Globalization of business activity

Since change has always characterized business activity, do these forces represent something new? Are the effects of change more severe now than in the past? The answer is *yes*—the forces of change operating on business organizations seem more powerful, disruptive, and faster moving than in the past.

One reason is that to survive, many organizations must undergo restructuring that is more extensive, more widespread, and more disruptive than was formerly common. In effect, many business firms are reinventing themselves to survive or to improve their competitive positions.

A second reason is that competitive success has become more short-lived than in the past. Success now seems based on the abilities to identify emerging customer preferences and to move faster than competitors to develop the products and services that customers will want in the future.

A third reason is that information resources play a more central role in organizational success than in the past. Long-term effectiveness requires continuously updated information on issues such as changing customer needs and developments in customer and supplier marketplaces. Success requires the ability to translate information into a stream of products and services that equals or surpasses that being developed by competitors. According to some observers, a business organization's only sustainable advantage is the ability to learn faster than its competitors.

The discussion that follows describes major ways in which organizations are changing. This chapter provides the context for discussing the emerging objectives of information resources in the insurance business and the criteria used to evaluate information resources.

Focus on Customer Satisfaction

Like other business firms, insurance organizations are redefining the concept of customer satisfaction. Previously, quality of products and services was largely viewed from the provider's point of view. The performance of a product or service was often judged against intended performance. Organizations presumed that their customers were being satisfied if the firm's sales goals were attained and if complaints were low. An insurer might have assumed that policyholders were satisfied with its claims service because the insurer met its contractual commitments and met its internal standards for the promptness of contact and the time required to settle claims. Similarly, agency staff members might have assumed that the agency provided adequate service if it could deliver policies to insureds as fast as competing agencies could and if few customers complained about its service.

In the past, organizations sought feedback by asking customers, in essence, "How do you like our products and services?" Organizations now also ask, "What products and services would you like us to provide?" Information about customer perceptions, opinions, and preferences, often obtained through marketing research, influence insurance organizations as they establish objectives and strategies.

Managing Information Resources

How insurance organizations handle automobile accident claims illustrates their recently intensified commitment to customer service. Traditionally, an insurance company or agency judged its claims service by measures such as the speed of initial contact and the time required for investigation and settlement. That traditional approach has been supplemented by a desire to understand satisfaction from the customer's point of view. Insureds might have very different views of the services they should receive. After a noninjury accident, some insureds might want to make a single toll-free call to the insurer and have the insurer immediately arrange for towing, taxi service, a rental car, and lodging or travel arrangements if necessary. To those insureds, customer satisfaction depends largely on the assistance received immediately after an accident. Other insureds might want other types of service, such as help in getting repair estimates and selecting a repair facility. Challenges for today's insurance organization include the following:

1. Determining what customers want and how present and potential customers define satisfactory service
2. Not gauging service by traditional measures based on the organization's work flow

Emphasis on Service

Property and liability insurance coverages are increasingly regarded as commodities by customers and by people in the insurance business. Personal lines policies have long been standardized, especially since they are often written on forms provided by rate advisory organizations. Some commercial coverages are also viewed as commodities now. If customers perceive a type of insurance as a commodity, they are likely to focus on price and service as the major purchase criteria. Many factors constrain an insurer's ability to adjust price or coverage and limit an agency's ability to secure a given coverage at a bargain price. In contrast to price inflexibility, insurers and agencies might have greater flexibility to improve customer service and to influence the customer's perception of that service.

Many insurance customers have infrequent contacts with their insurers or agencies. Because billing and payment are often done by mail, months and years might pass between events requiring service. Such customers might base their opinions about company or agency service on these infrequent contacts and on statements made by other customers. Any incident or report of poor service might be magnified in a customer's mind and might dominate the customer's perception of the company or agency. Information resources play an important role in the speed with which agencies and insurers respond to customer inquiries and thus influence the customer's perception of service.

Fast and complete response to customer inquiries requires on-line electronic access to needed information.

Consumers have become accustomed to having access to many services twenty-four hours a day and seven days a week. They order merchandise, arrange travel, and pay bills by telephone or by personal computer any time of the day or night. While in supermarkets and shopping malls, they stop at automatic teller machines to deposit or withdraw money from their bank accounts. Such round-the-clock convenience experienced elsewhere leads customers to think that they should be able to contact insurers, insurance agencies, or claims representatives outside of normal business hours. Moreover, customers increasingly expect to hear an insurance service representative say, "I have your file on the computer now" rather than, "Can I call you back on this?"

Focus on Core Business

In recent years, many insurance organizations have narrowed their market activities to those that they define as within their core businesses. Organizations have done this by selling off other products and services. Formerly, many large insurance organizations developed broad product lines, perhaps under the once-popular notion that "the financial supermarket" would dominate the marketplace for financial products. Many large insurance companies maintained broad product lines in the belief that agencies needed or favored insurers that could meet all of their coverage needs.

Focusing on core business areas indicates a commitment to customer satisfaction: organizations are now often willing to drop products and services in which they cannot excel. The insurance business's experience parallels that of other businesses and a general movement away from giant conglomerate organizations consisting of businesses that are not closely related.

Focusing on core business areas allows an organization to leverage its special competencies. For example, a firm with extensive loss control expertise can take greater advantage of this competency by selling loss control services to other organizations in addition to providing those services to its own insureds.

The Decline of Command and Control Management

The traditional management approach in most large organizations has been that of a tightly structured hierarchy, with highly defined jobs and top-down authority and control. This approach has been termed **command and control management.** In a command and control organization, employees follow highly detailed operating procedures in doing their jobs. A command and control organization is likely to have many management levels. As a result, managers have relatively limited spans of control and closely supervise employees. In such organizations, work flows and tasks rely on strict division of labor, detailed procedures, rules, and defined authority.

Among the disadvantages of command and control management is its rigidity. Change is difficult because employees perform jobs that tend to be limited in scope and inflexible. If the organization adds new products and the work becomes more complex, it must create additional procedures and rules. Managers then have more procedures and rules to monitor and enforce. Command and control management rarely taps the full energy, thinking power, or creative potential of employees. Although command and control management might succeed in a static environment or period of crisis, it is becoming inappropriate in today's fast-paced, competitive business environment.

Command and control management is still practiced in the business world in the United States and elsewhere. The trend, however, is to replace the command and control framework with new ways to achieve coordination: flexibility in job design, teamwork, and commitment to objectives. This trend has been visible in the insurance business as well as in many other businesses in the 1980s and 1990s.

In moving away from command and control management, organizations redefine the roles of managers and employees. Among the means used to reshape roles are the following:

- Replacing authoritarian controls with self-control
- Encouraging innovation
- Empowering employees

Information resources are essential if those changes are to succeed. Employees must have the information they need if they are to achieve objectives.

Replacing Management Control With Self-Control

Command and control management presumes that managers should perform the control function. Managers at all levels establish objectives and define how performance should be measured. The control function of an insurer or a major division of an insurer might involve overall measures such as the expense ratio, loss ratio, and combined ratio. Within an insurance agency or brokerage, managers might use overall results measures such as sales volume and commission revenue. Within a department or unit, performance measures might include compliance with budgets, productivity measures (such as policies per employee), processing time (such as average time to process an endorsement), and work backlogs. Such performance measures might be closely related to the organization's objectives. Results can be influenced by factors beyond the control of the individuals or units involved, such as catastrophes, the actions of competitors, and staff changes.

In eliminating command and control management, organizations develop ways for employees to measure and control their individual performance and, collectively, the performance of their teams, units, and departments. For example, objective performance measures obtained directly from the information system might supplement and/or replace subjective performance evaluations and feedback from one's boss. When possible, employees participate individually and collectively in the process of setting goals and defining the performance measures that will be used to evaluate success in reaching goals. This process is consistent with the general management framework known as Management By Objectives (MBO).

Coordinating at Lower Levels

In moving from command and control management, organizations seek to build direct coordination among employees, as contrasted with coordination through the hierarchy. Employees are urged to communicate directly with other employees to handle work flow problems. Communicating directly is faster and less prone to distortion than communicating up, across, and down the hierarchy. The job of the manager or supervisor changes from providing coordination to monitoring coordination and ensuring that coordinating processes are used and effective.

Empowering Employees

Empowerment is giving employees the power to make decisions without requesting the approval of the supervisor or manager. Work teams, task forces, and units, as well as individuals, can be empowered. In eliminating command and control management, organizations give employees and groups the right to make the immediate decisions required by their work. Empowerment often involves increasing the range of problems that employees can solve without obtaining advance approval.

In empowering employees, organizations stress the clarity of objectives and the quality of the information available to employees. Employee empowerment reflects the general trend of providing better customer service. Empowered employees can often solve problems for customers (and for other organization members) immediately.

When employees and groups are empowered, the job of the manager or supervisor shifts from making decisions to helping employees learn to make sound decisions. Managers and supervisors must provide support when decisions turn out to be wrong. They help employees to learn from their experiences and thus to make better decisions in the future.

Stimulating Innovation

Another aspect of the shift away from command and control thinking is encouraging employees to innovate. Innovation carries risk: not every innovation is successful. Indeed, if every innovation in an organization is a success, the organization is probably screening out many innovations that are worth trying. In some organizations, the penalties for a new idea's failure are so severe that they discourage employees from suggesting innovations that do not seem certain to succeed.

Encouraging innovation requires removing penalties for failure and giving employees recognition for all innovations, even those that turn out to be unsuccessful. Encouraging innovation also requires providing employees with the information they need to see problems and tasks in broader perspective. As with other aspects of the movement away from command and control management, the manager's role shifts from personally acting to ensuring that employees are equipped to act.

Closer Relationships With Suppliers and Customers

Suppliers of goods and services were traditionally regarded as outsiders. Maintaining a somewhat distant relationship with suppliers was considered desirable when negotiating with them. A more contemporary view is that vendors are business partners whose collaboration is valuable when problems are encountered. For example, an insurer contracts with body shops to provide service to insureds without competitive estimates. The insurer guarantees that the repair work will satisfy its insureds. To the insurer, the benefits of close coordination and joint problem solving outweigh any potential advantages of a more distant bargaining relationship with body shops.

To an independent insurance agency, insurance companies are suppliers. Agencies increasingly align their goals with those of the insurers they represent. Similarly, insurers value the opportunity to harmonize agency and company plans for business development.

Agency/company electronic interface provides efficient and accurate exchange of information, enhancing the business partner relationship. The same is true within the direct writing and exclusive agency distribution systems: electronic data interchange improves coordination and fosters partnership. Customers should benefit from closer agency/company partnerships. For example, insurers might give agencies greater underwriting and claims settlement authority than they would in the absence of the business partner relationship.

Outsourcing Products and Services

Insurance organizations are **outsourcing** or contracting other organizations to perform functions previously handled within the organization. Common examples are the company cafeteria being outsourced to a catering company and the corporate travel service being run by a travel agency. Once again, this trend mirrors what is happening in many business organizations and highlights the need for experience and expertise.

Some insurance organizations outsource part of their information service activities. The decision to outsource information processing might be more complex and difficult to analyze than the examples cited above. Maintaining effective information resources is a central function in an insurance organization, but the cafeteria and travel functions are not. Nonetheless, many insurance organizations have outsourced some information processing work in recent years.

Some organizations ask vendors to bid on automation projects in competition with their own information system departments. Perhaps the most common outsourcing of information processing activities involves computer operations. Application development (writing a new program) is also common. An organization is unlikely to outsource its entire application development function. Rather, a vendor might be hired to design and build a particular system.

Business Alignments

Rather than abandon a product line, a company might enter into an agreement with another company that specializes in that product. For example, an insurer lacking expertise in boiler and machinery insurance might purchase loss control and claims services for that line from another insurer possessing the competencies the first insurer lacks. The insurer purchasing the services might tailor its policies to conform to those of the specialty insurer. The insured might be unaware of the second insurer's involvement but will likely be pleased that a separate boiler and machinery policy would not be required. As insurance organizations concentrate more on their core businesses, the probability increases that such business alignments will become more common.

Globalization of Business Activity

The insurance business, like most other businesses, continues to globalize. Few products or services are not international: most use resources from and reach markets in many countries. Large insureds operate internationally and want their insurers and agencies or brokerages to provide service wherever they operate. Insurers merge or affiliate with insurers in other countries to expand their markets, to improve service to insureds, and to channel their growth into countries and regions with high growth potential. The globalization of insurance should continue in the years ahead. One consequence of globalization is the need for information systems that overcome problems of distance and differences in time and language.

The changes that have just been described are prevalent throughout the property and liability insurance business. They affect operations in agencies and brokerages as well as in insurance companies: they permeate insurance organizations of all sizes. Consequently, the requirements for success in the insurance business have shifted. One of those requirements, effective use of information resources, is particularly important.

Information Resources Objectives

Information resources are evolving in response to the changing business climate just described. In addition, improvements in information resources are being driven by other forces, including advances in automation technology. Among the objectives insurance organizations have in improving their information resources are the following:

- Improving the processing of work
- Improving product development
- Improving document delivery
- Improving decision making
- Measuring performance
- Achieving user focus rather than technology focus
- Developing inter-organizational information flows

Improving the Processing of Work

Organizations expect automation to significantly improve how they process their work. Faster information processing has always been an objective of information system projects. However, the way success is defined and measured has changed, and the scope of typical automation improvement projects has widened.

Insurance companies were among the earliest major users of computers. Their computer departments have typically been renamed every few years to reflect automation's maturing technology. Thus the Data Processing Department became the Electronic Data Processing Department, which became the Information System Department, or simply **Information Systems** (IS), which, in turn, became **Information Services** (also IS). This sequence of names suggests an evolution from a focus on the task being performed to the results achieved by the organization's use of information resources. The long evolutionary process of successful automation has progressed in the following way:

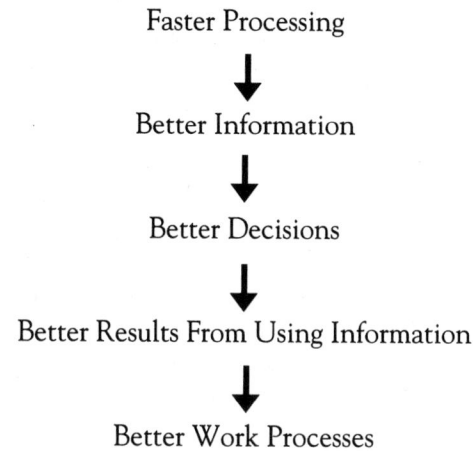

Information resources are now devoted to objectives that are greater in scope than those that were previously common. As mentioned, the emphasis now is on improving business processes so that they produce better results. Business processes are now defined as major activities rather than as single jobs, tasks, or parts of tasks. The processes include human as well as automated operations. Several units or departments could perform the operations that constitute a business process. Therefore, automation projects often involve several of the organization's units or departments.

Policy production illustrates the broadening scope of automation projects. In the past, an organization might have designed an automation project to reduce the time required to produce an insurance policy. The project involved a part of the information system known as the "policy production subsystem." Today, an automation project is likely to be designed to reduce the time required to process an application from the moment of sale through policy mailing. Such a project involves (using the traditional terminology) the underwriting, rating, and policy production subsystems. The project also involves agency/company interface and electronic data interchange with, for example, a motor vehicle department. Organizations now find focusing on changing their business processes more productive than changing the traditional subsystems of the overall information system.

The term **re-engineering** is often used for large-scale efforts to redesign major business processes. Re-engineering projects usually substantially or completely redesign jobs, work flows, and information flows within a segment of the organization. Re-engineering projects focus on business processes or products rather than on information subsystems. Re-engineering efforts often evaluate what is being done in addition to how well it is being done. Re-engineering might lead to massive changes that include restructuring the organization and downsizing, as well as changing tasks and procedures. Although many projects of this massive nature are called re-engineering, some do not use that label.

Improving Product Development

Recognizing the need to be more responsive to emerging customer needs, insurance organizations seek to improve their product development procedures. For agencies and brokerages, product development is more likely to involve offering new services than new products. For convenience, this section will use the term **product development** to include completely new products, significantly modified products, new and modified services, and entry into new regions or markets. Improving product development requires improving data access and decision support tools as well as reducing the time needed to bring a new product to market.

Data Access

Designing a new insurance product or service usually requires access to vast amounts of data. Rate advisory and statistical reporting organizations provide aggregate data that are useful in analyzing a proposed product's market potential. Organizations also extract data from their own databases to evaluate a new product's sales potential. The IS department faces the challenge of retrieving data in ways that might not have been contemplated when the database and system were designed.

Pollution liability policies illustrate the challenge of obtaining information for new product development. Several years ago, the need for pollution liability insurance became evident, but no such product existed. Little data was available that could be used for product design, pricing, and underwriting. Some relevant data did exist in the records of claims made under existing policies. The data located there included paid claims and claims not paid because the exposure was not contemplated when the policy was written. Insurers had difficulty extracting those data from their files because that need was not envisioned during system design. IS professionals now design greater data access capabilities into insurance databases.

Analytical Tools

Many staff members are involved in designing new products, modifying existing products, developing underwriting guidelines and rates, and designing marketing programs for new products. Those staff members can use increasingly powerful and sophisticated software for data analysis and modeling. The software allows them to extract data from huge databases, analyze the data, and perform "what-if" analyses to model the outcomes of various assumptions and decisions.

Purchased software is often used for data retrieval and analysis. Powerful software packages allow users to perform data analyses that previously required the assistance of expert programmers. Users benefit by getting results faster and by being able to ask new questions immediately after they see initial results. The ability to ask new questions is especially valuable because initial results rarely provide sufficient information on which to base a decision. The role of the IS department includes the following tasks:

- Developing or selecting the analytical software
- Tailoring it to users' needs
- Providing training in using the software
- Performing retrieval and analysis that users are unable to perform

Product Introduction Time

A common goal in improving information resources is to reduce the time required to create and market a new product or service. This time is often called "product launch time" or "time to market."

Many steps are involved in launching a new insurance product or service. In addition to providing data analysis and outcome modeling for product design, mentioned above, automated tools assist in designing the work processes that will produce and deliver the new product. Automation is typically used in creating support materials for training employees in the tasks they will perform with a new product. The support material might include on-line help screens for those who work on the new product.

Effectively using information resources can speed up the many steps in product development and launch. Integrated computer aided software engineering (ICASE) tools and object-oriented programming are two of the software tools that reduce the programmer time required to create programs. Those tools are described in Chapter 2.

Efforts to reduce product launch time are often complicated by the need to design the processing system along with the product. The design of an insurance product might require the design (or redesign) of the tasks, forms, work flows, and information flows that would be used in providing the product. An insurer might find that the only way to market a proposed commercial coverage profitably is to design a streamlined production process for its underwriting and policy issue.

Improving Document Delivery

The process of producing and delivering the insurance policy has traditionally been a bottleneck in the insurance work flow. "Delivering," in this sense, refers to producing the policy documents. Physical delivery might be accomplished through an agency or directly to the insured.

In the past, it was not unusual for an insurance company to have errors in over 30 percent of the policies it produced. Policy production was primarily a process of assembling paper documents. Information was entered on separately printed forms, and the necessary forms were combined to constitute the policy. Errors could occur in entering the information on the paper forms and in assembling the forms.

Laser printers and associated software have made it practical to print an entire policy on plain paper rather than to assemble it from a series of printed documents. Similarly, laser printers within agencies have made it economical to create documents by entering information electronically rather than by typing it on printed forms. Insurance organizations use electronic form creation to produce certificates and other documents in addition to the insurance policy.

Error rates typically decrease when electronic form creation replaces the traditional process of entering information on printed forms. The computer system that creates the forms can be programmed to check many items as they are being entered. Although laser printing has greatly improved document preparation, insurance organizations seek further improvements in document preparation and delivery. One such improvement will occur as information now located on paper documents becomes available directly from expanded databases.

Improving Decision Making

Another contemporary objective of information resources development is to improve decision-making processes throughout the organization. As previously noted, many organizations want to empower employees at all levels. Empowering employees requires giving them the information they need as well as the authority to make decisions.

Local area network (LAN) technology dominates insurance organizations. In a LAN system, workstations throughout a location are interconnected so that they can share data and software. The workstations are personal computers that store data and programs. Before LANs, many insurance workstations were terminals, which are input/output devices that do not store data and programs. LAN workstations give users control over the data and programs that they use frequently. LANs also give access to data that might be created and stored elsewhere in the information system. LANs are described in greater detail in Chapter 2.

Within the insurance business, LANs supplement but do not replace the giant computers known as "mainframes." Only mainframe computers can contain the huge databases necessary for the operations of insurance companies and large agencies. Only mainframes can provide efficiency in performing major processing runs, often called "production runs." Since mainframe computers are connected to LANs, local area networks combine the mainframe's efficiency in performing large tasks with the speed and convenience of processing small tasks on the user's computer.

Insurance organizations capitalize on LAN technology to improve decision making by buying and developing software designed to improve data analysis and report writing. The software facilitates data retrieval, data analysis, graphic presentation of results, and preparation of reports. For example, the organization can provide standard spreadsheet forms called "templates" for specific applications. Templates often eliminate the need for staff members to create their own spreadsheets. Templates also facilitate aggregating data into unit, departmental, and organizational totals.

Measuring Performance

Automated information systems often provide measurements of performance. Those measures typically report performance at many levels: units, departments, divisions, territories, and the entire organization. Systems can also report performance on other bases, such as the performance of specific products, services, and marketing programs.

Effective performance measures should have the following two characteristics:

- *Objectives-based*—should measure activities in ways that are consistent with the organization's objectives.
- *Acceptable*—should be seen as valid and appropriate by those whose results are being measured. New organizational objectives often require developing new measures.

The term **information overkill** describes the situation in which an information system measures too many things and produces reports that overwhelm users with detail. The management information systems of the past often resulted in information overkill, and managers often complained that important facts were difficult to find in a sea of information. Focusing on major organizational objectives should reduce the number of performance measures that an organization uses but could also intensify the challenges of tailoring performance measures to current objectives and making them acceptable to those whose performance is being measured.

Product development time is an important performance measure in many insurance organizations. As mentioned earlier, insurance organizations are trying to reduce the time required to launch new products. They also want to reduce the time required to tailor an existing product to meet an individual customer's requirements. (Commercial lines policies for large accounts often contain many manuscript endorsements that tailor coverage to a customer's needs.) The organization's information system should provide feedback on the time needed to tailor products to customer needs as well as on the time required to launch new products and services.

Since customer service is a major concern of insurance organizations, their information systems might be programmed to measure the processing time for tasks such as policy issue, endorsement processing, and claim handling. Those measurements are often made on a unit and departmental basis. Many computer systems can measure the productivity of individuals whose work is system-based. Some organizations choose not to use this system capability. Among the reasons for not using individual productivity measurements is the fear that some employees will sacrifice quality for volume and will neglect nonmeasured work to concentrate on measured activity. In addition, some organizations believe that machine-made measurements of individual performance conflict with the organization's desired culture and management style.

Achieving User Focus Rather Than Technology Focus

Information resources continue to decrease in cost. When computers and programming were considered to be expensive, system development decisions necessarily had a technology focus. IS executives wanted to make the best use of expensive resources, programmer time, and machine time. Recently, hardware and software costs have dropped, and programming has become far more efficient than in the past. Consequently, organizations have been able to shift the focus of development from technology to users' needs.

In focusing on users' needs, IS staff members study how employees actually use information instead of how they are supposed to use it. The same is true for how employees use computer systems. System designers now try to provide screens that give users the information they want in the sequence and form in which they want it. For example, a computer screen can display an exact replica of a paper form. To the user who enters information into the form, having identical paper and electronic forms is very convenient. The user can follow identical processes for the electronic and paper versions of the form. Focusing on users' needs when designing automated information systems improves productivity, reduces error rates, and makes training easier.

Organizations use several structures to ensure user participation when developing information resources. These structures include the following:

- Steering committees
- Department automation committees
- System managers
- Automation meetings

Steering Committee

A large insurance organization is likely to have an automation **steering committee** to establish long-range plans for developing information resources. The steering committee studies the entire organization's emerging information needs. The steering committee also helps to establish information resources objectives and applies these objectives in recommending proposed projects for approval. An automation steering committee is usually headed by one of the top executives in the organization. Executives of several line departments as well as IS executives also serve on the committee.

Department Automation Committee

In large insurance organizations, major divisions or departments might have their own automation steering committees. These committees assess needs and assist in planning and coordinating automation projects within their departments. Like a steering committee, a department automation committee might recommend approval of proposed projects and might assign or recommend priority rankings for approved projects.

System Manager

The term **system manager** generally identifies the person responsible for an automated system within a user organization. The person who serves as system manager might have other duties and might have a different job title. For example, an insurance agency's system manager might be called the "operations manager," "automation manager," "system coordinator," or "office manager."

System managers perform many system-related duties including troubleshooting, training, recording system malfunctions, and running automation meetings.

Project Teams

Installing new and replacement automation usually involves a **project team**. Often, a separate team will be created for each automation project. The team might consist of the system manager, users, and IS specialists. The project team does the following:

- Investigates the need for a new or modified system
- Researches design alternatives
- Recommends a system for development or acquisition
- Obtains management approval at appropriate stages of a project

Automation Meetings

Periodic automation meetings play an important role in the day-to-day management of information resources. Participants are either all system users or, in large units, representative system users. The system manager usually runs an automation meeting, and the manager or supervisor of the unit should attend. Automation meetings allow users to identify problems, develop solutions, discuss needs, and share tips for using the system.

Developing Inter-Organizational Information Flows

Insurance organizations can lower their processing costs if paper communication is replaced by direct data exchange with other firms. Many of the paper documents sent from one organization to another are created by a computer and convey data to be entered into the computer of the other organization. But having the computers exchange the data directly, at least with routine transactions, is more efficient. This direct computer-to-computer data exchange between organizations is known as **electronic data interchange (EDI)**.

Processing glass claims illustrates how organizations use EDI. An insurance company might contract with a glass company to handle its glass claims. The insured is given a toll-free telephone number to call with a glass claim. A customer service representative in the glass company answers the insured's call. The representative accesses the insured's policy file, verifies coverage, and makes an appointment at a glass shop convenient to the insured. The appointment message includes coverage information, so further coverage verification is unnecessary when the insured arrives at the glass shop. When the work is performed, a glass shop employee enters the information in the shop's computer. The information is transmitted to the glass company and, in turn, to the insurer. The insurer's policy record is updated with the closed claim information. The glass company sends an electronic invoice each month to the insurance company. The invoice contains information about the work done by each shop during the month. The insurer pays the invoice electronically, and the insurer's bank transfers the funds from the insurer's account to the glass company's account.

EDI standards also foster electronic communication between insurance organizations and insureds. For example, an employee of a manufacturing company might mail a workers compensation claim directly to an insurer. If EDI standards are used and if the organizations interface, the claims representative can access the personnel files of the manufacturer to verify that the claimant is a covered employee. Security provisions protect employee privacy by restricting the data that the insurer can access.

Adopting EDI standards also facilitates electronic communication between insureds and their agencies or brokerages. Risk managers of large organizations might use computer systems known as "risk management systems." Interface allows risk managers to use their risk management systems for routine communications such as reporting information that might affect coverage, requesting certificates, or checking the status of claims.

Insurance organizations exchange vast amounts of data with each other, with suppliers and customers, with statistical and other service organizations, with regulators, and with other organizations. The potential for cost savings through EDI is substantial. Moreover, EDI offers the promise of better relationships with other organizations by engaging in cooperative action and by reducing problems such as data errors and delays in transmitting documents. For those reasons, insurance organizations actively participate in national and international efforts to develop EDI standards. Those efforts are described in Chapter 3.

Information Resources Evaluation

How should an insurance organization assess the effectiveness of its information resources? Traditionally, information resources were evaluated by determining cost savings and the degree to which processes were automated. Such tests of effectiveness are no longer sufficient because of the changing business climate and the emerging objectives for information resources. In addition to cost-effectiveness, insurance organizations now evaluate the effectiveness of information resources by also considering success in attaining project and system development objectives, user satisfaction, user involvement, and the integration of information resources planning with strategic planning.

Cost-Effectiveness

Cost-effectiveness remains a conspicuous objective as insurance organizations manage the development of their information resources. Organization and department steering committees consider cost-effectiveness when making long-range plans to develop and use information and when relating information resources to organizational objectives. Steering committees also use cost/benefit analysis when evaluating proposed information projects and assigning priorities to approved projects. Chapter 3 discusses the cost/benefit analysis of information projects.

As previously suggested, the concept of effectiveness is changing. In the past, organizations tended to define "effectiveness" as the value of the information produced by automated systems or as the technological capabilities of the information systems. Organizations are now more likely to link information system effectiveness more closely to the achievement of organizational objectives. At the organizational level, these objectives are strategic and long-range and are often expressed by competitive performance and return on funds invested in the organization. At lower levels, such as at the department level, objectives could be stated in such terms as sales volume, growth, customer service, and the profitability of specific products and activities. Clearly, achieving such objectives is influenced by many factors in addition to information resources.

Nonetheless, organizations want to explicitly link information resources and organizational results. One framework for describing the linkage is to state how information resources contribute to the distinctive competencies that produce organizational results. For example, an insurer might develop skill in underwriting professional liability insurance as a distinctive competency. The insurer might define "effectiveness" (in evaluating cost-effectiveness) as successfully using knowledge-based underwriting systems in processing professional liability applications.

Project Objectives

Organizations evaluate the success of automation projects by the degree to which project objectives are met. The success of each project should be evaluated by the project team, the department automation committee, and the steering committee. Department automation committees and the steering committee should also review the success of a series of projects. That review might be performed annually. As part of their planning and control activities, line executives should review the committees' evaluations.

System Development Objectives

Another criterion of overall information effectiveness is success in meeting the objectives of long-range system development plans. Those objectives might be expressed as information resources capabilities. For example, an insurance brokerage might establish an objective of achieving interface with its fifty largest clients in three years. Success in meeting the goals of a new technology implementation plan, described in Chapter 2, is also considered in judging the attainment of system development objectives.

The steering committee should periodically evaluate the organization's success in achieving its system development plan. Senior executives should review the steering committee's evaluations as the senior executives fulfill their control responsibilities and as they make strategic plans for the organization.

User Satisfaction

Another criterion used in evaluating the effectiveness of information resources is the extent to which users believe their needs are being met. A thorough analysis of user satisfaction should consider two components:

1. Satisfaction with the existing system
2. Existence of unmet needs

Members of IS departments obtain feedback on existing information resources through informal discussions and through more formal means such as questionnaires, interviews, and focus groups. IS departments also obtain valuable information by analyzing users' requests for help from IS staff members and from help desks.

IS staff members should periodically ask users to identify needs that are not being met by the existing system. To elicit this information, IS interviewers can ask users to identify obstacles that prevent users from doing better work. Interviewers can also ask users to describe ideal information resources for their jobs and departments.

User Involvement

Many insurance organizations want to develop a partnership between information services professionals and the users they serve. This sense of partnership goes well beyond the idea of user satisfaction. User involvement is evidenced by true collaboration of users and IS professionals in steering committees and project work. It is also evidenced by a flow of suggestions from users to IS and by the openness of communication between users and IS staff members.

Integration With Strategic Planning

Because insurance is an information-intensive business, developing information resources should be integrated with developing strategic plans. When businesses started using them, computers and information were seen as productive resources similar to raw materials. They were to be purchased in whatever quantities would produce the desired output. The organization set its business plans and, as a supporting activity, developed or acquired the productive resources needed to accomplish the plans.

Information resources are no longer considered productive resources in the traditional sense. Instead, information resources constitute an insurance organization's competitive strength. Information and the ability to use those resources open some paths and close others in planning the organization's future. The ability to create and use information could profoundly influence the design, pricing, and marketing of new products or services. In many cases, the information resources must be in place before a product or service can be launched.

Improvements in information resources should continue in the years ahead. In particular, insurance organizations should achieve progressively greater integration of the technologies described in this chapter. By focusing on business results rather than on technology, organizations will provide their own incentives for creative and integrative changes to their information resources.

How can an organization evaluate the extent to which it has integrated information resources planning and strategic planning? If the two elements are integrated, they occur together and not in a means-end relationship or as successive steps. If they are integrated, the same executives and managers are involved in strategic planning and planning for future information resources. If information resources planning and strategic planning are integrated, they use the same time horizons. Any vision of what the organization should be in five or ten years must include a vision of the information resources of the organization at that time.

Summary

Information is the paramount tool for doing insurance work. Insurance organizations need effective information resources if they are to survive and succeed. Information resources must respond to visible changes throughout the business world. Change characterizes the business world, yet the changes occurring now seem more severe and more urgent than in the past. The expected life span of competitive success seems to have permanently shortened.

Among the forces that are reshaping the business world is a focus on customer satisfaction, with particular emphasis on providing services that customers now desire. To meet customers' needs, many organizations are reducing the scope of their activities and are focusing on what they define as the core business. To excel within the domain of the core business, many organizations are defining new roles for themselves and new relationships with other organizations. Business alignments provide opportunities to combine the strengths and competencies of separate organizations. Outsourcing currently is a popular way for an organization to leverage its energies and talents. In outsourcing, other organizations are hired to perform some activities that were previously handled within the organization. Insurance firms sometimes outsource information processing and information system development activities.

Concurrent with the changes that are making organizations more focused and customer-driven are the changes occurring in the management of business organizations. The command and control organization model of the past is becoming less appropriate for today's organizations. In moving from command and control management, organizations are replacing managerial control with self-control, fostering coordination at lower levels rather than through the hierarchy, empowering employees, and stimulating innovation. Those changes will not succeed if the organization fails to develop effective information resources

Efforts to improve information resources focus on several objectives. In general, insurance organizations are developing their information resources in ways that allow them to improve work processes, accelerate product development and document delivery, improve decision making, measure organizational performance, and communicate efficiently with other organizations. Users play an increasingly prominent role in the evolution of information resources, and a focus on users' needs is replacing the technology focus that was previously common.

In response to changes in the business climate and information resources objectives, changes are occurring in the evaluation of information resources. The traditional measures of automation success were cutting costs and expanding the amount of automated work. More contemporary measures include success in achieving project and system development objectives, cost-effectiveness, user satisfaction, user involvement, and the integration of information resources planning with strategic planning.

Chapter 2

Information Technologies

This chapter describes some information technologies gaining importance in helping insurance organizations make optimal use of their information resources. The technology wheel in Exhibit 2-1 provides a framework for categorizing the technologies described here. This categorization is not exact, since some technologies do not fit precisely into any one category. Potential applications, business implications, and benefits of each of the technologies are also discussed in this chapter.

Image Processing

The insurance business has always been inundated with paper, from correspondence, policies, and claims to computer-generated reports. Although some of this paper can be discarded, some of it must be retained to meet legal requirements and the need for later reference. Paper flow must be managed throughout the paper's life cycle, including receipt, duplication, distribution, indexing, filing, tracking, and retrieval. Managing paper has a number of problems that impede productivity, including the following:

- Response is slow when the document is requested.
- Requested documents might be lost, misfiled, or damaged.

Exhibit 2-1
Technology Wheel

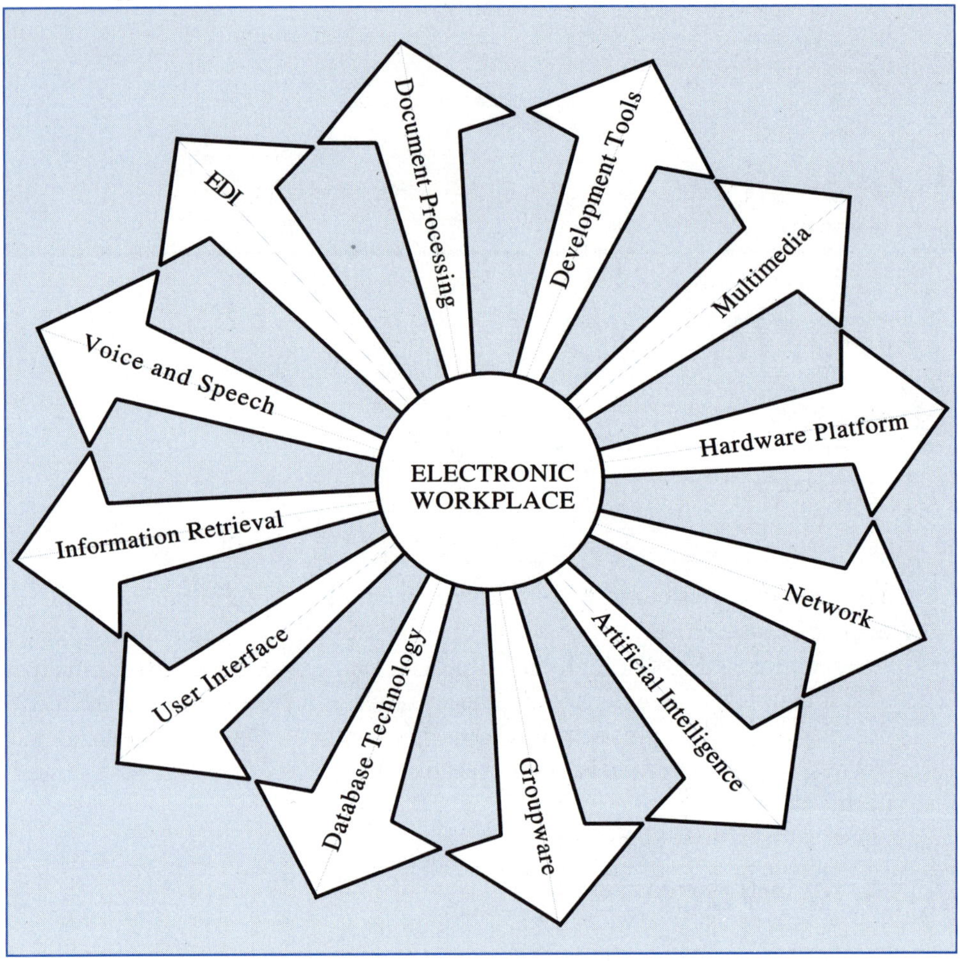
Document Processing
Development Tools
EDI
Multimedia
Voice and Speech
Hardware Platform
ELECTRONIC WORKPLACE
Information Retrieval
Network
User Interface
Database Technology
Artificial Intelligence
Groupware

- Manual filing is labor- and space-intensive.
- Only one person at a time can access a document unless copies are made.

Image Processing Technology

Imaging is the process of converting information on paper into a computerized digital format using a scanner, facsimile machine, or other device. The two broad applications of image processing are:

- Storage and retrieval applications
- Image processing applications

Storage and retrieval image applications provide electronic document management for correspondence, policy and claims files, contracts, and litigation support. Image processing applications include processing new business applications, endorsements, and premium payment transactions.

Advantages

Advantages associated with storage and retrieval applications include the following:

- Files are almost always available and complete.
- Database access and search programs provide greater flexibility and ease in finding files and records than do manual file searches.
- Storage space requirements are reduced.
- Lost and misplaced files are eliminated.
- Security is improved.
- Many people can view a file at the same time.

Advantages of using image processing applications include the following:

- Productivity is increased.
- Operator pacing is improved.
- Paper handling is reduced.

Components

Image processing systems include the following components:

- **Scanners**—to copy the document into an optical image.
- **Indexing workstations**—personal computers to assign one or more indexes to the scanned image before it is written to a disk. Although indexes can be generated automatically using bar codes and optical character recognition of specific fields, the most common method of creating indexes is manual entry.
- Optical disk storage devices—for long-term retention. Most optical disk drives use **write once, read many (WORM) technology**. Once the number of scanned images exceeds the capacity of a single platter, most organizations use devices known as "jukeboxes" to rotate stored disks into position for reading and writing.
- Software—to compress images before they are stored, manage indexes, control the storage devices, and manage work flow based on criteria established for each document.

- Image-capable PC monitors or terminals—required for image retrieval workstations.
- Optical character recognition and optical mark recognition equipment—required if the application will be extracting data from scanned images for data entry or indexing documents.
- Laser printers—to print images.
- Fax gateways—allow image systems to receive and send images to and from remote sites without the need for a hard copy.[1]

Challenges

Image processing projects present a number of challenges. Computer phobia and fear of job loss have always been concerns of employees whenever automation projects are planned and implemented. Education, user involvement throughout a project, and positive experiences with new technologies in other areas of the organization can overcome those concerns.

Legal evidence rules and signature requirements determine how much paper can actually be eliminated. The same rules that currently apply to microfilm and other storage media also apply to documents stored and retrieved using imaging processing. The best way to determine legal requirements is to consult with the company's or agency's attorney.

Work process redesign should be based on business objectives, not on electronic imaging processing technology. Other factors critical to the success of an image processing project include the reliability of the image hardware and software, the system's ease of use by the casual user, user training, and the ability to integrate the image system with conventional data supported by the company's or agency's existing hardware and software.

Business Implications

Initially, image processing was seen as an extension of microfiche technology that improved the efficiency of storing and retrieving large volumes of documents. However, image processing has a fundamental advantage of allowing the processing of a document's contents to be separated from physical paper management. The need to handle the same document at different locations has been a major source of inefficiency. Documents are lost or located in the wrong place; creating and storing duplicates represent substantial overhead; and if documents are subject to revision, different versions inevitably result. Image processing used in local area and wide area networks can overcome those problems. Work flows can be redesigned to allow different departments to process a document's contents simultaneously rather than sequentially. Documents can be managed at a central location and distributed electronically to where they are needed. If documents are printed, the printed versions can be automatically dated and time-stamped to ensure version control.

Application Development Tools and Techniques

Traditional methods used to develop insurance company and agency automation systems are changing. The huge mainframe-based computer systems developed during the last thirty years are reaching the end of their useful lives. Many of those systems are too large and complex to be redesigned. Revising them might require using old and inefficient languages and methods. Organizations cannot afford to wait for traditional, multi-year development projects to be completed. With the competitive environment rapidly changing, traditionally developed systems might be outdated by the time they are implemented. To reduce the time for new products and services to reach the market, insurance organizations use new application development tools to create and maintain more flexible systems in less time than was previously possible.

Rapid Application Development

Rapid application development (RAD) describes techniques that reduce the time between system specifications and the final testing of a new computer program. Joint development teams and prototyping are two of the most commonly used RAD techniques. **Joint development teams** are composed of business and systems specialists who work to complete a given project. **Prototyping** is a technique used to build a quick and rough, but real and executable, version of a system or part of a system. Since the prototype illustrates the system to the members of the joint development team, it allows the team to identify flaws in its original approach and invent ways to improve the system. Prototypes allow system users to review their proposed interactions with the system in a hands-on manner rather than to review paper specifications. Managers can assess the project's progress at any time simply by running the prototype rather than reading extensive documentation on work in progress.

Reusable Code

Architects can plan a house from an existing design that they modify, or they can assemble a plan from separate, existing designs. Until the introduction of interchangeable parts that could be assembled into a rifle by skilled workers, guns were individually handcrafted. Introducing interchangeable parts made the workers more productive. Building new information systems from existing documentation, designs, and code reduces development time. The term **code** means a computer program or a portion of a program. A programmer writes code, and a computer program consists of lines of code.

Information services departments can store software modules in indexed libraries and can reuse the modules in new systems. Reusable parts can be developed in-house or purchased from outside software vendors. To be successful, this approach requires development groups to find the right **reusable code** (for each of several files to be read), to fit the reusable code to the new system's requirements (combine data in new ways), to distinguish among similar but different functions, and to write and classify new pieces of reusable code.

Integrated Computer Aided Software Engineering

Generating application software in a series of seamless steps starting with an automated graphical model of the process to be automated and moving through prototyping, system design, automated program generation, and system testing should be possible. This is the goal of **integrated computer aided software engineering (ICASE)** tool vendors. Other ICASE goals include the following:

- Development of higher-quality systems that meet business and processing objectives
- Increased flexibility to move applications to the most cost-effective hardware and software as technologies change
- Faster development of business systems by reusing prior system designs to allow an organization to take advantage of market opportunities

If used in the traditional life cycle method of systems development, ICASE tools do little to reduce the amount of time required to develop applications. In the traditional system development life cycle method, development occurs in the following stages:

- Requirements definition
- Function specification
- Design
- Programming
- Testing
- Implementation

The requirements definition stage finalizes the systems specification as early as possible so that the functional specification stage can begin. The functional specification stage outlines the functions necessary for the system to meet the specifications outlined in the requirements stage. Following the functional specification stage, the detailed design stage occurs. In this stage, the functions are described in great detail. Programming and testing precede implementation. Maintenance follows implementation. However, making significant changes in the requirements is usually difficult and time-consuming because systems are usually not initially designed to accommodate major subsequent modifications. An evolutionary or iterative system development life cycle coupled with an ICASE tool allows developers to work with requirements for the start of a project and to meet new requirements during the life of the application.

A variation of the reusable code concept previously discussed is using existing code in the form of packaged application software. Adapting conventional packages to support an organization's current work flows or redesigned business processes is difficult because most packaged application software is not designed to meet special needs. Software packages developed using ICASE are highly reusable, and they are sold as designs rather than as computer code. Once the design has been modified to meet the organization's business requirements and work flows, the design can be processed by an ICASE tool's code generation component.

Object-Oriented Programming

Most traditional programming languages, such as COBOL, BASIC, Pascal, and C, are sequential. Programs written in those languages are long lists of precise instructions that the computer follows exactly as they are written. Each instruction usually performs a single operation such as reading, writing, or adding one piece of datum to another. Because the instructions are steps in a procedure, those languages are called "procedural languages."

In contrast, an object-oriented program does not consist solely of a precise sequence of instructions. Instead, an object-oriented program defines a framework within which a program's objects are to behave. An **object** is a simulation of any real-world object. Examples of objects within the insurance business include a window on the computer's screen, an insured's file, an auto insurance policy, and a claim file. An object consists of data and the operations that can act against it. When an object-oriented program runs, a relatively small list of instructions route program execution through the framework. The objects come to life: a window appears on the computer screen; an insured adds a new driver or changes coverages and automobiles; a claim file issues periodic payments; or reserves change based on current data.

The major goals of object-oriented programming are as follows:

- Reusability—objects are designed so that other programmers will use them to build systems.
- Simplicity—programmers deal with objects rather than pages of program code.
- Control of complexity—objects of growing complexity can be built from other, simpler objects.
- Rapid design—applications can be constructed from existing components or objects.
- Quality design—applications can be built from well-tested components.
- Simplified maintenance—an object can be modified without affecting other objects.

Hardware Platforms

Computing hardware continues to evolve. Advances in microchip technology enable hardware manufacturers to reduce the computer's physical size while increasing its processing power. New methods of interacting with and entering data into computers are also being developed.

Local and Wide Area Networks

Until the 1980s, the mainframe was the primary component of the information system of most insurance companies and large agencies. Terminals and distributed processors were regarded as secondary components in the system. By the end of the 1980s, this situation had changed. Employees had acquired powerful personal computers that could contain software and sizable databases. Employees reaped the benefits of having greater control over the data and the software they used regularly. To get the most from their PCs, employees wanted to access data and programs stored in the mainframe and in other PCs. They also wanted access to plotters, scanners, printers, and other input/output devices. By connecting PCs, local area networks changed PCs from machines that worked in isolation to devices that gave access to huge databases and promoted teamwork in using information resources.

A **local area network (LAN)** connects computers and other devices in a small area, such as in an office, in a building, or in adjacent buildings. The devices in a LAN are connected by a cable or fiber-optic link. A **wide area network (WAN)** covers larger distances (relative to a LAN) and transmits data by microwave or other means. LANs and WANs usually function within an organization. Connections with other organizations are more likely to occur by interface or electronic data interchange, which will be discussed later in this chapter. The value of LANs and WANs in an organization comes from their ability to link many hardware and software products in a single system.

A local area network can become overloaded and, consequently, can increase computer response time. Limiting the number of workstations on a network reduces the likelihood of overload. Workstations that interact frequently can be connected to LANs. The LANs can be linked with a backbone network using special hardware and software. Exhibit 2-2 shows a backbone network that links LANs and a WAN.

Exhibit 2-2
Network with Multiple LANs

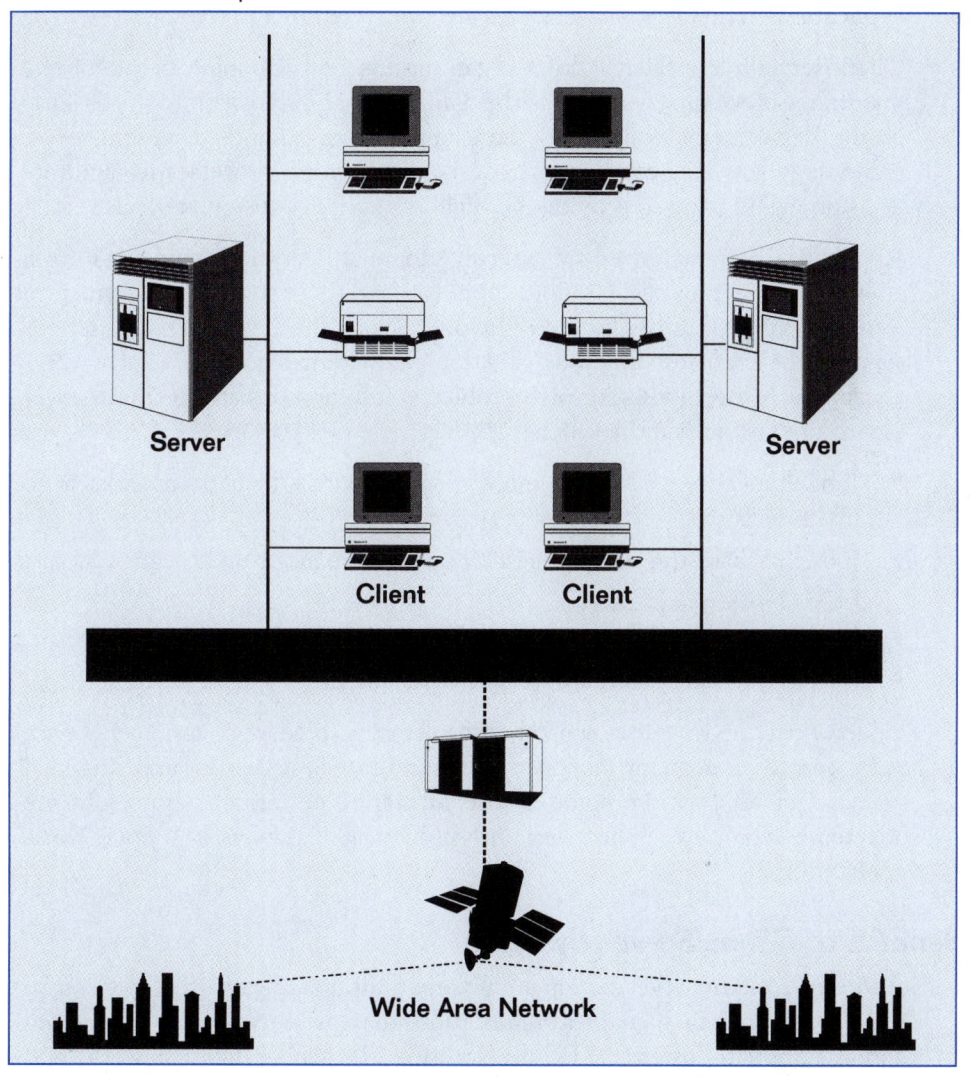

Client/Server Systems

The system or style of computing that has developed in conjunction with intraorganizational networks is client/server computing. In a **client/server system**, the network is the system. Instead of running on a large mainframe, applications are distributed across many computers called **clients** and **servers**. **Clients** are the personal workstations in the network, and **servers** are the computers that run the network. Clients can access any other computer system or server on the network to obtain data, an image, or any other resources needed from a database. Clients can also send or receive faxes. The user sees a common graphical interface that provides access to all necessary business applications. The clients and servers are connected in a LAN.

Client/server technology allows organizations to take some or all of the mainframe processing work out of the data center and transfer it to the desktop or the department where it is more appropriately handled. Client/server technology acts as a catalyst for redesigning business processes to facilitate decision making and to provide the highest quality of customer service.

Applications characterized by extensive manual operations gain little from client/server technology. Complex applications, those that require some professional expertise, provide greater payoffs because the graphical user interface supports the event-driven processing that characterizes how knowledge workers approach their jobs and solve problems. Jobs appropriate to client/server environments include the following:

- Jobs that require access to multiple data sources to perform tasks or to make decisions
- Jobs that base the next request or series of requests on the answers just received
- Jobs that result in a decision or action
- Jobs that require assimilation skill or judgment

Underwriters, underwriting support staff members, producers, customer service representatives, account managers, claim adjusters, actuaries, and financial and budget analysts are some of the insurance personnel whose jobs are affected by complex applications and sophisticated systems to support those applications.

Benefits of Client/Server Systems

Adopting a client/server system allows organizations to gain greater access to company-wide data. It enables organizations to implement flexible, integrated applications with lower-cost PCs. In addition, the availability of powerful and easy-to-use development tools promotes the rapid development of high-quality and affordable new systems. But adopting a client/server model is challenging.

Challenges of Client/Server Systems

Moving from a mainframe-centered to a client/server system requires significant changes in how people think about information technology. In a client/server system, the user must be an integral part of the application development process rather than a passive recipient of it. Application design and development methods must include the user, take advantage of new software development tools, and incorporate prototyping approaches in the system development process. Also, staff members who design new software must develop skills to ensure reliable and efficient communication among the different computers connected by the client/server system.

To help guarantee integration and flexibility, all applications must be implemented under the umbrella of clearly defined and broadly accepted principles and development standards. Choosing those principles and standards involves trade-offs, and enforcing them can be difficult. Like mainframes, client/server systems need protection from entry by hackers, vandals, and thieves. Security software to control access in multi-site client/server environments is not as functional or long-lived as that used to control access to mainframes.

Client/server systems require system management facilities found on the mainframes, such as software version control and data storage and processor management. Client/server systems also require additional facilities, such as network planning, network monitoring, and fault recovery procedures for the local area network.

Another concern associated with client/server systems is data backup and client recovery. Most users keep their data in their local client computers. Therefore, a mechanism for regular backup and client recovery is crucial. Detailed planning and implementation of a client backup strategy are necessary to lessen the risk of data loss.

Components of Client/Server Systems

Client systems usually include intelligent workstations connected to a local area network through software and network interface cards in each workstation. Servers are networked computers providing clients with services such as database access, transaction processing, connection to a host (mainframe) computer, printing, and image processing. Servers are task-specific and can range in hardware from inexpensive PCs to mainframes. Networks contain a variety of hardware and software components that link clients, servers, and local area networks to each other and to the external world. Business-oriented software helps implement daily tasks and processes. Application software includes groupware, work flow facilitation software, spreadsheets, word processors, and tools for analysis and reporting. System management components manage the network and telecommunications software, provide backup and recovery, and monitor system performance.

Advances in computer power and networking technology led to the creation of peer-to-peer networks. In a traditional client/server environment, clients depend on servers for activities such as printing and communication with other clients. In a peer-to-peer network, each client can act as a client and a server. Thus, every machine on the network has the same data communication capabilities as every other machine. If a server is unavailable, client machines, acting as both clients and servers, can function with their full array of features, whereas in a traditional client/server environment, they might not.

Parallel Processing

Parallel processing has been used since the first multiprocessors and nonstop minicomputers appeared in the 1970s. **Parallel processors** are computers that have many central processing units (a personal computer has one) working together. The scientific community uses parallel processors for the high-volume, high-speed processing required for such complex tasks as weather forecasting. Parallel processors are also used as database servers, primarily for large databases and complex decision-support applications making up data warehouse applications, which will be discussed shortly. Parallel processors are also used for high-volume, on-line transaction processing applications such as automatic teller machines and airline reservation systems.

Pen-Based Computers

Pen-based computers are small, tablet-like devices that use an electronic pen (called a "stylus") for input rather than or in addition to a keyboard or mouse. Pen-based computers come in many forms. They provide a keyboard for data entry, while tablet computers do not. Palmtop computers are small, lightweight devices that fit in the user's hand. Pen-based computers can be connected to desktop computers for applications that do not require mobility.

Pen-based computing is used to perform functions such as claims adjusting, loss control inspections, sales, premium auditing, and other field activities. Pen-based computers can communicate data gathered in the field to computers in other locations through built-in modems and telephone lines.

Benefits of Pen-Based Computers

Pen-based computers provide the following benefits:

- The ability to collect and provide information to others, either data collected in the field (from loss control to underwriting) or data accessed in the field (such as claim adjuster access of policy data or claim status).
- The ability to obtain complete and accurate information. Data can be collected when entered, and the originator can check for errors.
- The ability to save money by reducing or eliminating clerical data-entry support.
- The ability to increase efficiency and productivity. For example, loss control representatives might be able to make more inspections if they are able to complete their inspection reports on-site rather than wait until they return to the office.[2]

Challenges of Pen-Based Computers

Challenges in developing and implementing pen-based applications include the following:

- Although graphic fields or designated areas of the screen can be used to capture signatures, text, and drawings, the technology to translate handwriting into typewritten text is relatively crude.
- Integrating hundreds or thousands of pen-based systems in the field with existing systems requires coordinating communications and synchronizing application software on those devices.
- More complex applications such as insurance policy preparation and sales force automation already available on the mainframe or client/server systems cannot use pen-based technology without extensively converting or rewriting the applications to run on pen-based computer operating systems.

Artificial Intelligence Applications

Artificial intelligence (AI) allows computer hardware and software to imitate the operation of the human brain. AI applications, such as playing chess, use computers to analyze situations (all potential moves the opponent might make) and reach decisions (the next chess piece to move). Several types of AI systems are used to develop applications in insurance organizations. **Knowledge-based systems, neural network**s, and **case-based reasoning** are examples of such AI applications.

Knowledge-Based Systems

Knowledge-based systems (KBS) try to make computer hardware and software imitate how people reach decisions in specific situations. Knowledge-based systems have three components:

1. Database
2. Knowledge base
3. Control program called an "inference engine"

The database contains background information about the field of expertise and specific information about the particular situation to be evaluated. For example, a database for an underwriting KBS might include new business applications, credit reports, motor vehicle reports for each driver, and claim history files.

The knowledge base contains the set of rules experts use to make decisions or recommendations using database information. The rules are developed by a careful and extensive study of how selected individuals make specific decisions. The persons selected in creating early KBS applications were the most expert within the organization. Early KBS applications were called **expert systems** because they captured and modeled the reasoning of experts.

Knowledge-based system rules are *if/then statements*, such as the following:

IF (vehicle_too_old AND not_enough_driving_experience)
THEN consider_referral.

Although if/then statements are used in traditional procedural languages, expert system languages do not require that if/then statements be organized in a specific sequence. Using data from a database or from a system user who enters data through a workstation, the control program or inference engine searches for the rule that applies (vehicle too old AND not enough driving experience calculation rule, for example), uses the rule, and searches for an additional applicable rule (consider referral rule), uses it, and so on until a conclusion is reached.

Applications of Knowledge-Based Systems

Insurance organizations use knowledge-based systems to arrange and analyze information and to solve problems. Knowledge-based systems are well adapted for applications that require giving advice, searching, interpreting, predicting, explaining, data mining, diagnosing, configuring, scheduling, monitoring, and planning. Practical insurance applications of knowledge-based systems include fraud and benefit misuse detection, underwriting, work flow control, structured settlement calculations, case reserving, cross-marketing analysis, actuarial modeling, and customer support groups providing problem-solving assistance to system users.

Benefits of Knowledge-Based Systems

Benefits traditionally associated with knowledge-based systems include enhanced quality and accuracy of decision making and reduced dependence on subject matter experts within the company, especially if those experts are expensive or in short supply. Many organizations now find greater benefits in applying knowledge-based systems to automate competency rather than expertise. These systems are able to automate many of the routine and repetitive decisions required to process new business, claims, and renewals. The result is increased productivity and responsibility because employees are freed to analyze and oversee more complex tasks.

Neural Networks

Neural network software, sometimes referred to as **adaptive systems**, can make decisions in much the same way people do. Neural networks get their name from the number of interconnected nodes in each of the input, processing, and output layers, as shown in Exhibit 2-3. The processing layer is where "learning" in the form of pattern recognition takes place. Learning occurs through trial and error, just as it does for people. A neural network's ability to identify patterns in data makes it ideal for generating useful information from existing databases. This ability, known as **data mining**, helps extract additional value from existing data. After information in the form of histories is extracted from the database, the neural network software recognizes patterns that make the information more useful in decision making. For example, in order to identify desirable policyholder characteristics, the software could identify patterns in insurance applications, policy data, motor vehicle reports, credit reports, and claim data. As another example, the software could identify patterns in claim data to detect potentially fraudulent workers compensation claims.

Case-Based Reasoning

When confronted with a new problem, people often rely on the success and failure of past attempts (or cases) to solve problems similar to the one at hand. **Case-based reasoning** attempts to model that thought process. According to case-based reasoning, the best expert should be the person with the most experiences or cases to draw on. A person who has solved a similar problem before might be the best one to solve a current problem.

A case is a description of a problem, an attempted solution, and the outcome of the effort. A case base is an accumulated body of problem-solving experi-

Exhibit 2-3
Neural Net Nodes and Layers

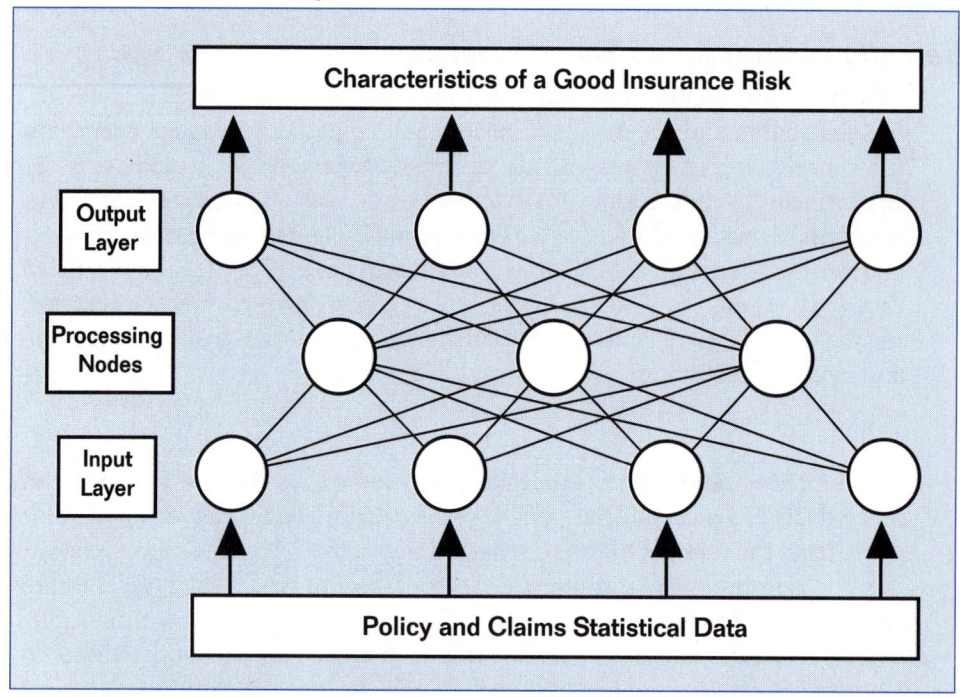

Characteristics of a Good Insurance Risk

Output Layer

Processing Nodes

Input Layer

Policy and Claims Statistical Data

ences. As the cases increase in size and diversity, the case base becomes more useful, especially to people who have not had similar experiences. For example, help desk applications become more effective each time a problem is reported and its solution is entered into the application's case base. Case-based reasoning systems can help staff projects and product development teams determine what past projects relate to the requirements of the new one. Other potential applications include underwriting risk evaluation and classification, proposal development, and legal reasoning.

Groupware

Work groups are not always physically located near the manager or supervisor. Some work groups or members of work groups are geographically dispersed, working at home part of the time. Other work groups, such as those developing industry standards, have cross-organizational boundaries. Maintaining work group competency and achieving team work are particular challenges when team members or employees are dispersed. Knowledge is lost when a member leaves the group. New members usually need time to reach the performance level of other group members.

The term **groupware** describes applications designed to overcome the challenges noted above by providing electronic support for groups of individuals working together toward common goals. Groupware applications can be classified as systems supporting communication, cooperation, and coordination. Communication-oriented groupware applications, such as electronic mail and calendar scheduling systems, result in an action only when requested by an individual user. Cooperation-oriented applications support group member interaction around shared document databases, such as reference libraries, jointly authored documents, on-line conferences, tracking of critical issues, and policy formulation. Coordination-oriented applications support group completion of a specific process such as transaction processing or project management.

Graphical User Interfaces

The two major ways in which users enter instructions into a computer are through keyboard commands and through screen symbols called "icons." For example, in command-based interaction, the user presses a series or combination of keys to instruct the computer to print a document. In a **graphical user interface (GUI)**, the user positions an arrow on a printer symbol (icon) and clicks on the mouse button to tell the computer to print the document. The initial motivation behind graphical user interface was to make the computer emulate work as people performed it in real life. Experience has shown that a GUI leads to higher productivity and less frustration than character-based, command line interfaces used in mainframe terminal-based applications.

Components

Components of a solid graphical user interface include the following:

- A *desktop* control function that allows users to conveniently arrange icons for programs and files on the screen
- *Windows, icons,* and an *action bar* containing pulldown menus that allow the system user to select the next function to perform and do it without procedural restrictions imposed by the program
- *What you see is what you get* (WYSIWYG) presentation
- *Business terminology* rather than computer jargon

Graphical user interface supports multiple, parallel paths of work for users, allowing them to work in many different applications just as they would work with many different folders on their desks. Windowing permits users to move quickly among different tasks just as users have been able to view different parts of a paper file in the past. As powerful as graphical user interfaces are, they do not guarantee a system that is user-friendly or easy to use.

User-Friendly Systems

One of the consistent themes in systems development is making systems easy to use and easy to learn to use. The trend in systems development is toward client/server systems that use graphical user interfaces such as Microsoft's Windows. Well-designed graphical user interfaces help users learn their systems faster, make fewer errors, work more productively, spend less time training, and concentrate on the work to be done rather than on how to use the system.

Installing a Windows-based or other graphical user interface application does not guarantee a user-friendly system. The first step in developing a user-friendly system is to set a measurable objective. In an application used by customer service representatives working with customers over the telephone, the objective is to complete the transaction quickly without the need for a call back. The next step in creating a user-friendly system is to identify objects and actions associated with the business function. Graphical user interfaces can be developed using object-oriented programming languages described earlier in the chapter.

Exhibit 2-4 contrasts a traditional mainframe/terminal-based application with a Windows-based application. The mainframe application presents a series of screens. Each asks the system user to make a decision. Once the decision is made, the system user is usually asked in the next screen to make another decision to retrieve the desired information. The user must page through the file in search of the needed information. If related information from other files is required, another page-by-page search must be completed.

Using the Windows-based interface model, the user immediately begins working with information—in this example, the files for three insureds. All three sets of files can be displayed simultaneously on the screen, and the user can move around in each and move back and forth among them. This illustration is an example of what is meant by "working with information, not the application."

Ease of Use

Increasingly, systems are used outside of the organizations in which they originated. Usability of insurance company systems is a competitive advantage when providing systems and interface to other organizations. In addition to GUIs, the following also affect a system's ease of use and the ease of learning to use it:

- The software installation process
- On-line tutorials and other training aids

Exhibit 2-4
Contrasting Terminal Presentation Styles

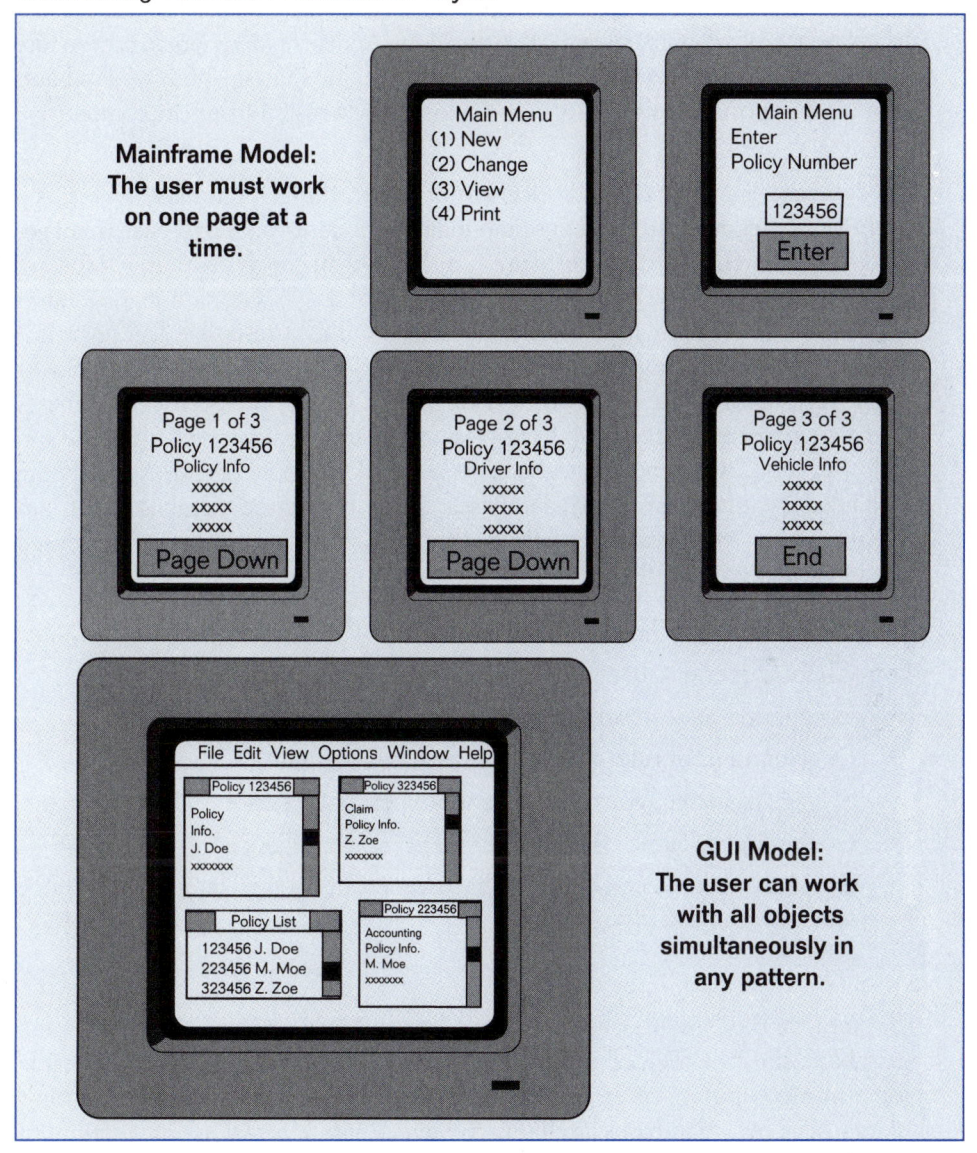

- On-line help in the form of step-by-step instructions on how to accomplish a task
- Error recovery instructions identifying the problem and explaining how to correct it
- Compatibility with existing systems

Database Technology

The quantity of data stored and the complexity of data organization are ever-increasing for an insurance organization. The management of databases plays an important role in decision-making practices and thus in competitive success.

A **database** is an organized collection of stored files. A database serves as a central library of information used in many applications. A **database management system (DBMS)** is a software tool that organizes the data in a database and establishes the procedures for data retrieval. Early database management systems placed files in a hierarchical arrangement that resembled an organization chart. Proceeding through each information block to reach the blocks that were subordinate to it was necessary. These early hierarchical databases were supplanted by relational databases that cross-referenced file data and allowed more direct access to data. Relational databases, in turn, are being replaced by object-oriented databases. Object-oriented databases contain objects, data structures, and methods that allow the data structures to be used and modified efficiently.

Database management systems should support the following:

- Client/server database applications
- Compound data structures such as spreadsheets and tables
- Development of rules for knowledge-based systems
- Storage of image, voice, video, and unformatted text
- Compound documents containing text, voice, video, and images
- Rapid database access such as that needed in agency/company interface systems

Distributed Databases

To achieve the benefits of client/server systems, large, monolithic mainframe databases must be divided into several databases, each small enough to reside on a minicomputer server dedicated to providing access to an organization's database. Those databases are likely to have separate locations. A distributed database is a collection of separate processing and database server sites connected in a data communications network. A person who seeks data should not have to be concerned with the data's location. Data stored in multiple locations must be synchronized across all servers so that the integrity of the data is maintained. The data might be in one or in a combined version of the following forms:

- Distributed—data elements are divided among each of the servers at each site.
- Replicated—multiple copies of the same data elements are contained on several distributed servers.

Control, as well as the data, is distributed so that operations can continue despite communication or processing failures at a given site.

Data might be distributed by territory, function, resources, or responsibility. Since every multi-site organization has a working method for distributing critical files, any effort to change the location of files usually begins by determining where and how paper and automated files are currently stored. Does the company keep the records for its California business in its California office, or are all records stored in the home office?

Distributed data are commonly used in a particular part of the organization, and most of the changes made to the data are generated by the staff in that part of the organization. Other parts of the organization usually have a low level of demand for data access and for detailed analysis of data from separate sites. Properly distributing data minimizes the need to access data stored in other parts of the organization and thus the influence of distributed databases on overall system performance.

Advantages

Advantages of distributed databases include the following:

- Data can be stored and accessed in a pattern that mirrors the organizational structure.
- Distributing data improves overall system resilience. The loss of one database or storage site does not affect the operation of applications using databases in other locations. If data replication is used, temporary operation is possible until full recovery is completed.
- Distributing data helps in managing large volumes of data.
- Distributed databases can expand individually as needed to support the growth of data.
- Response time and data availability are good if data elements are distributed to allow local access.

Distributed Database Issues

Management issues associated with distributed databases include the following:

- How closely should the distributed database match the company's organizational structure?

- Should data or just the access to the data be distributed?
- To what extent should control over the data be local?
- What is the cost of replicated data compared to the cost of lost time and poor customer service during the time required to recover or restore unavailable data?

Information Retrieval

Employees at all levels of an organization are often frustrated because they cannot access or have difficulty accessing needed information. The term **management information systems (MIS)** was used many years ago to describe what was then a new type of software application designed to provide information to managers and to perform transaction processing for operational departments. Management information system applications did not always meet expectations because most MIS systems were primarily designed to process new business applications, endorsements, payments, and other insurance transactions.

Management information systems were replaced by decision support systems designed around information needs related to decisions made by an organization's managers and executives. **Decision support systems** were supposed to become the tools that would automate managers and knowledge workers because those systems would do the following:

- Support group analysis and decision making by providing users with the ability to define decision criteria, perform individual quantitative analysis, and produce computer-generated results representing a group decision
- Allow "what if" and goal-seeking analyses of financial models

Decision support systems were regarded as more successful than most MIS applications. Financial analysts, business planners, and middle managers, rather than senior managers, were the primary users of decision support systems.

Executive information systems (EIS) evolved from decision support systems. An EIS is designed to meet the information needs of top executives. An EIS includes economic, financial, and other data from outside the organization. To be effective, an EIS user interface must be easy to learn and use. The user need not know the location of data elements or the computer languages used to retrieve those elements. Few senior level executives have the time to work with complicated systems. The information available to the EIS must be updated on a regular basis without any intervention by the system's users. The EIS must present information consistently throughout the company.

The system is designed to present and communicate information rather than merely to manipulate transaction-oriented data. Some of the information an EIS provides includes the following:

- Information and news on predefined subjects from external news services
- Sets of predefined reports and briefing books containing graphs and documents that can be reviewed in any order
- Exception reports identifying data or information that falls outside a predetermined range for a particular business objective or critical business performance factor
- The ability to select data fields from the organization's databases on an ad hoc basis and to create custom reports and graphs

In most organizations, information flows up to the top through various management levels, giving each level a chance to understand and react to variances. Since EIS systems provide senior management with information as soon as it is available, they bypass the traditional bottom-up information flow. The key factor in creating successful EIS applications is ensuring that executives, managers, and others simultaneously have access to the same data so that when the phone rings, lower-level managers, if they have reviewed the latest information available on the EIS, can be ready to answer "Why did this happen?" questions.

Voice and Speech Technologies

Computers no longer require access by computer terminals. **Voice response systems** enable customers with touch-tone telephones to communicate directly with an insurance organization's computer and to receive a response via digitized or synthetic voice. Such systems are used to answer insureds' questions about billing notices. They can also be used to refer a prospect to the closest agency or a policyholder to the nearest claim office. For example, a caller searching for claim assistance far from home can dial an 800 number and enter the ZIP or telephone area code of his or her location using the telephone's touch-tone key pad. The system will search the company's office and adjuster locations, select the most appropriate one, and then "speak" the name, address, and telephone number of the office if the caller does not want to be immediately transferred to an adjuster.

Insurance organizations employ other request and response systems besides the voice request/computer response system just described. Technology now supports the following:

- Voice request with paper response mailed to the caller

- Touch-tone telephone requests for information with the response faxed to the caller
- Voice messages stored in client and claim files along with text files and images of correspondence, policy documents, and accident information

Electronic Data Interchange

Electronic data interchange (EDI) is a general term for electronic communication in which two or more organizations, for example, insurance companies and their agencies, exchange business transaction data in structured formats that can be processed by computers. EDI is fundamentally a standardization of information formats among businesses. EDI is accomplished by agreeing on standard data communication methods and standard formats to transmit, accept, and understand business data. The term **interface** could be used as a synonym for EDI, but in the insurance business, "interface" usually refers to agency/company electronic communication.

Elements of EDI

The basic elements of EDI include the following:

- Intercompany communications. EDI links organizations and their customers and suppliers in a cooperative relationship that offers the potential for improving service and productivity. Data elements are exchanged electronically, in machine-readable form, without the need for manual intervention in data entry or conversion of data from one trading partner's format to the others. Networks link computers within each of the participating organizations, called "trading partners."
- Transmission of business documents. Business documents, rather than messages or narrative reports, are the substance of EDI transmissions. Typical documents include new business applications, first notices of loss, endorsements, invoices, and payment notifications.
- Formatted data. Carefully defined formats specify the order of data items in a transmission and the characteristics of each item to ensure that the data elements are received and properly understood.
- Technological transparency. Hardware, communication protocols, and data format differences are handled by translators on the EDI network or through software at each site. The user does not "see" EDI in use.

The EDI network interconnects the trading partners, either directly (that is, computer to computer) or indirectly by electronic mailboxes. Exhibit 2-5 shows the flow of information among organizations using electronic mailboxes. Located within a network, a mailbox holds documents transmitted from a source authorized to add to its contents. Documents remain in the mailbox until they are checked and retrieved by the mailbox holder. Network capabilities include transporting documents, routing, and security.

Exhibit 2-5
EDI Information Flow

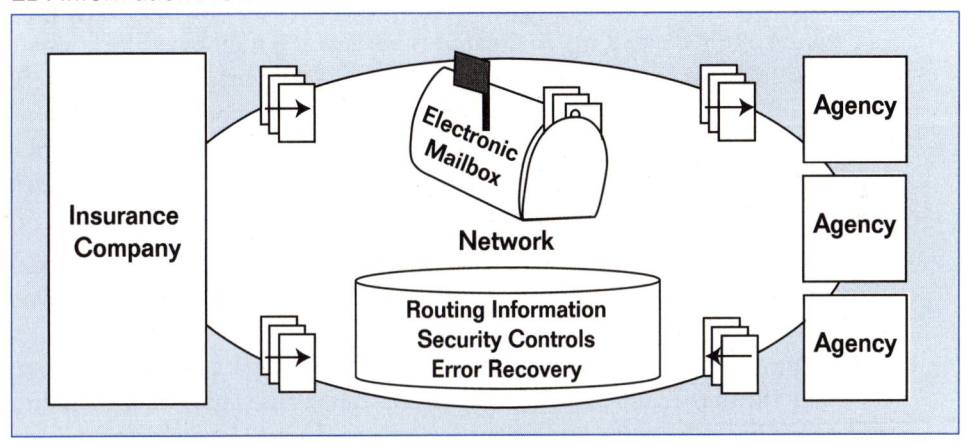

Benefits of EDI

The insurance business has a number of characteristics that have long made EDI an attractive technology. Substantial time is lost as paper travels between agencies and companies. The management of paper flow within companies and agencies is expensive and involves many people. Customer service standards within the insurance business are very high. Because of those characteristics, insurance organizations often include in their objectives improving organizational productivity and reducing the number of paper documents processed manually.

The major benefits of EDI are the speed of transaction processing, reduction of errors, rapid detection of errors when they occur, and reduction of paper documents. A great deal of computer output, such as that from an agency's computer system, often becomes input to another computer or several computers. For example, an agency might ask several insurance companies to provide quotes. In addition to the cost associated with the entry and reentry of data, a chance of error exists each time data elements are manually entered into a system. Computer-to-computer transmission of business documents not only eliminates costs but also eliminates errors that result from multiple data entry. Some errors might not stem from data entry mistakes but could result from differing business records such as the most current rates or coverages available from a company. EDI produces substantial cost savings. More important, the cost savings continue for every transaction and grow as business volume increases.

Industry Standards

In EDI, standard data formats prescribe the contents of a business transaction such as an auto insurance application and specify the content, order, and form of data to be transmitted. Some organizations develop their own EDI communication standards and require all of their trading partners to use them. Proprietary EDI systems limit the number of organizations with which an organization can communicate. Some agencies and other trading partners might be unwilling to adopt an insurer's proprietary interface system or to use a separate system for each insurance company they represent.

Standards define how the electronic documents are packaged and transmitted. Business documents transmitted by EDI methods are included in an "envelope" that contains the data as well as identification and routing protocols. The communications transport protocol specifies the procedures and speeds used to send the documents through various networks. This enables sending and receiving computers to coordinate transmissions. Interchange control segments identify a set of documents transmitted between organizations at one time. Within each transmission, headers and trailers separate the business data from the protocols.

Standards for insurance EDI have been developed on national and international levels. Insurance organizations participate in EDI standards-setting efforts directly and through **Agency-Company Organization for Research and Development (ACORD)**. ACORD is a not-for-profit organization created in 1970 to develop standards for exchanging data between property and liability insurance companies and independent insurance agents. For years, ACORD has developed paper forms and electronic standards for agency/company interface. Its involvement in EDI standards-setting indicates a broader role in electronic communication in the insurance business.

EDI Software

EDI networks use several levels of software. The communications software connects the sender and receiver systems to the transmission network and provides proper transmission procedures and speeds. Translation software transforms data from one form, such as that on the agency's computer, to another form, such as that used by a company. For organizations using EDI internationally, translation software also transforms one national standard to another.

Common Data Dictionary

A data dictionary specifies the number of characters or digits allowed for each item. The property and liability insurance business, through ACORD, has created a common dictionary of standards that is constantly updated.

Network Transmission Source

The transmission network might be proprietary, established for the sole use of an insurance company, or it might be for general insurance business use, such as the Insurance Value Added Network Services (IVANS) network. As Chapter 3 will discuss, the IVANS network is designed for use throughout the U.S. insurance business. The acronym IVANS stands for the network and for the organization that provides it. Even though the trend is moving away from proprietary systems, it does not appear certain that companies and agencies will use only a single network.

EDI Issues

As insurance organizations implement EDI, they must address the following issues:

- How can reinsurers, agents, regulators, banks, and other insurance company trading partners be encouraged to use EDI?
- How can the company or agency change how it does business in order to achieve the benefits of EDI?
- Should standard or proprietary methods be used?
- How will the cost of implementing EDI be shared with the organization's trading partners?

Multimedia

The idea of combining text, images, video, voice, and other types of sound with a user-friendly interface for education and marketing applications has been popular for some time. A system that does this is usually known as "multimedia." In the past, such systems faced storage capacity and processing power limitations. Today's powerful PCs overcome those problems. The availability of graphical user interfaces on PCs has also increased multimedia applications. The ability to provide remote multimedia displays is particularly important in providing unstaffed sales kiosks to the public, as the following example illustrates. If a customer is interested in shopping for auto insurance, the customer selects the auto insurance option on the kiosk's screen. After the customer reviews questions similar to the one illustrated in Exhibit 2-6 and

52 Managing Information Resources

responds by voice or use of a keyboard or mouse, a quote is developed. To buy a policy, the customer uses a telephone at the kiosk to establish a connection to an agency located in the community. The video screen in the booth lights up to display a picture of an agency staff member, with the insured's picture showing on the agent's screen. While the agency staff member completes the sales procedure and collects additional information to supplement that used to prepare the quote, the agency staff member can take an image of the customer's drivers license through another camera. After the application has been completed and displayed to the customer, the customer "signs" the application using a pen or stylus, pays by passing a credit card through the card reader, and obtains the policy or binder from the kiosk's printer. Such an "agent in a box" allows agents and companies to increase the number of marketing locations without adding staff or conducting business in locations that do not generate a large enough clientele to justify staffed service.

Exhibit 2-6
Insurance Kiosk Screen

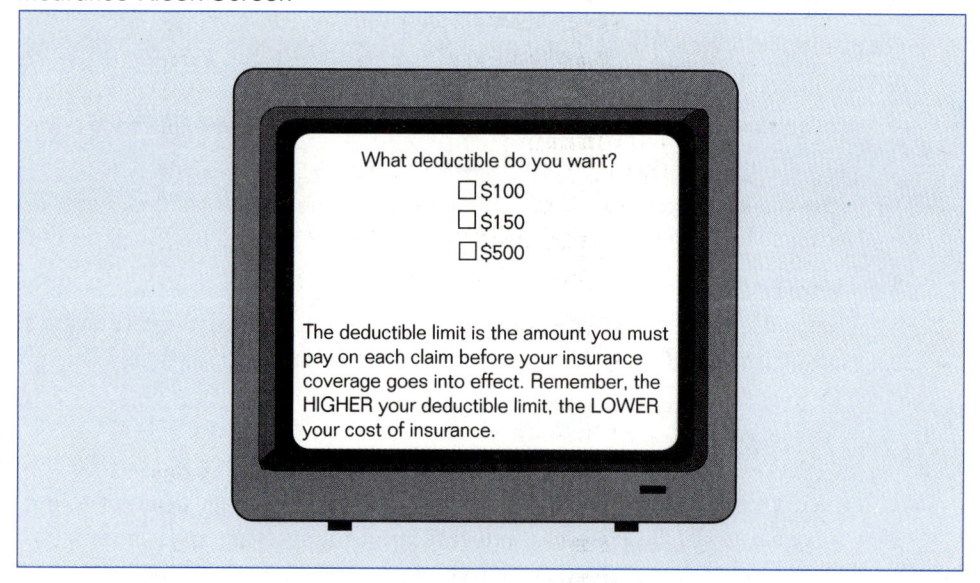

Implementing New Technologies

New technology eventually affects nearly all parts of an organization and almost always represents a significant cost to achieve the projected benefits. Because of this, the first major milestone in any new technology implementation project is to gain the support of executives and managers. Making a successful case for executive and managerial support requires a clear understanding of the project's costs and benefits. Once executives and managers are convinced of the match between the need for and benefit of the new technology, the new technology project can be started.

Executive and Managerial Support

Gaining support from the organization's executives and managers to implement new technology requires that the technology and potential projects using the technology are presented in a business rather than a technical context. Managers and system professionals who want to obtain approval for new technology should do the following:

- Express the expected results in terms of organizational objectives. Identify the manager's business unit objectives and performance targets, and then relate the technology to those objectives and targets. For example, if the business unit's objectives include reducing expenses, knowledge-based systems can be defined as technology that will directly achieve that objective by decreasing hiring and training costs.
- Understand the technology project in business terms, and express it that way. Implementing an image system can replace microfilm and reduce off-site storage costs. However, those results might not be as important as enabling users to immediately access underwriting and claim documents so that responses to customer inquiries are immediate and result in higher levels of service and increased customer satisfaction.
- Identify what the organization's key competitors are doing. Are they innovating? Are they doing things better? How do their expense and premium-per-employee ratios, for example, compare to those of the organization?

New Technology Implementation Plan

Improvements to automated information systems are generally made on a project basis. Projects are usually initiated for one of two reasons: to solve a work flow problem or to implement a long-range system development plan. Some of the projects resulting from an organization's system development plan are designed to control and coordinate new technology. For example, large organizations might have a new technology implementation plan to introduce new technology at a predetermined pace. The management of automation projects will be discussed in Chapter 3. The following discussion focuses on the new technology implementation plan that some organizations follow in managing the introduction of technologies such as those described in this chapter.

Ideally, new technology is implemented without any major problems. Otherwise, problems in initial implementation might be used by those critical or skeptical of the new technology to limit or stall further projects. The following four steps can help minimize problems in adopting a new technology:

- Plan the implementation. This step includes planning to acquire the hardware and software needed to implement the new technology, devising tests of the new technology, identifying pilot projects, selecting the staff, developing training plans for the pilot project team, and defining the expected benefits.

- Install and test the technology. The new technology should be evaluated before being pilot-tested in the organization. The testing process should reveal the strengths, weaknesses, and most appropriate applications of the new technology. Some advance tailoring of the product being installed might be necessary for it to function properly in the organization's hardware and software environment. Involving a member of the pilot project team in the installation and testing of the new technology is helpful. If problems occur during the pilot project, that team member's experience should be valuable in identifying the causes of problems.

- Conduct a pilot project of the new technology. A pilot project is not simply a test but is meant to be a permanent installation. A pilot project is selected and structured to allow the organization to evaluate results and revise the system or work procedures before using the system elsewhere. To champion the new technology throughout the organization, the project leader must be a good communicator and motivator. The project leader will also be responsible for monitoring and reporting on the progress of the pilot project. Chapter 3 will discuss automation projects.

- Review or evaluate the test and pilot project. The purpose of this step is to evaluate how well the pilot project was carried out and how well the technology performed versus its expected performance. Plans for continued implementation of the technology should be updated to reflect the assessment of the pilot project.

Applications

The following examples illustrate successful applications of new information technologies in insurance.

Automated Service Facility

Exhibit 2-7 contrasts the traditional customer access methods with the intelligent customer call center and an **automated service facility** or "clerk in a

Chapter 2 / Information Technologies   55

box" that can provide callers or users with twenty-four-hour availability seven days a week to solve problems or to obtain needed information.

Exhibit 2-7
Automated Service Facility

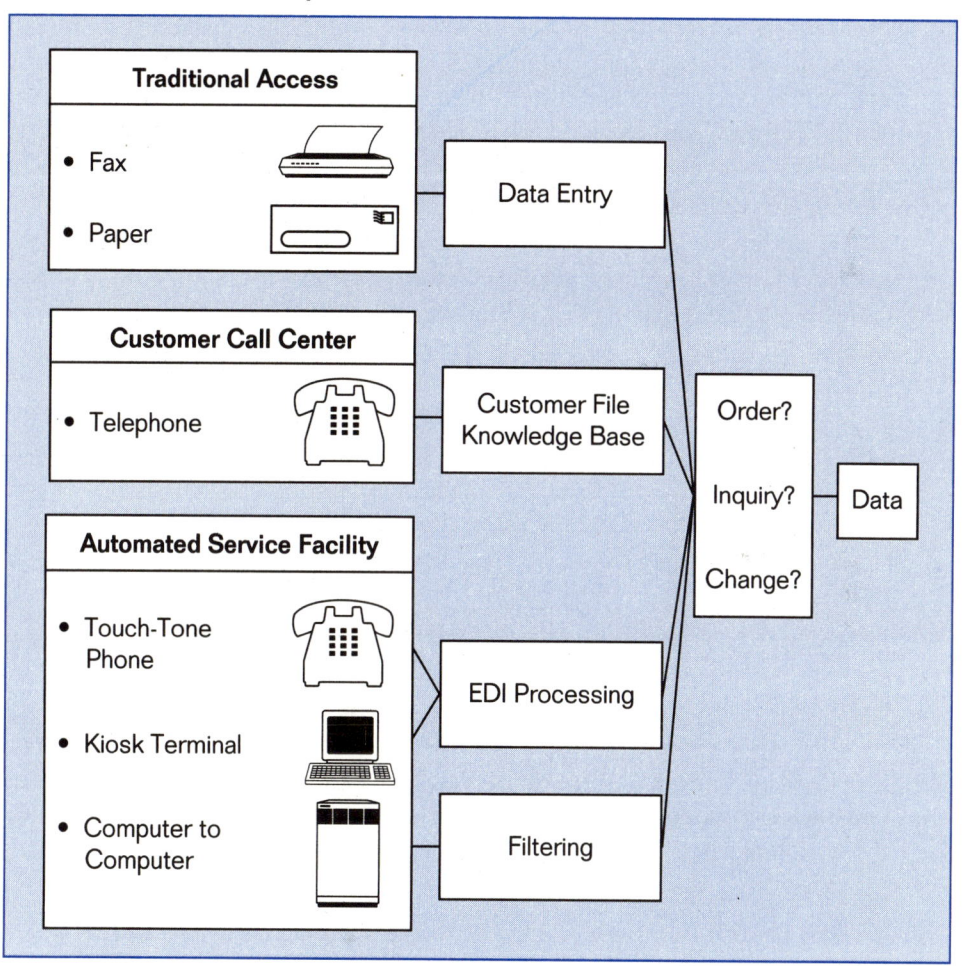

```
┌─────────────────────────────────────────────────────────────────┐
│  ┌─────────────────────────────┐                                │
│  │     Traditional Access      │                                │
│  ├─────────────────────────────┤   ┌──────────────┐             │
│  │  • Fax                      │──▶│  Data Entry  │─┐           │
│  │  • Paper                    │   └──────────────┘ │           │
│  └─────────────────────────────┘                    │           │
│                                                     │           │
│  ┌─────────────────────────────┐                    ▼           │
│  │    Customer Call Center     │   ┌──────────────┐  ┌────────┐ │
│  ├─────────────────────────────┤   │ Customer File│  │Order?  │ │
│  │  • Telephone                │──▶│Knowledge Base│─▶│Inquiry?│▶│ Data │
│  └─────────────────────────────┘   └──────────────┘  │Change? │ │
│                                                      └────────┘ │
│  ┌─────────────────────────────┐                    ▲           │
│  │  Automated Service Facility │                    │           │
│  ├─────────────────────────────┤   ┌──────────────┐ │           │
│  │  • Touch-Tone Phone         │──▶│EDI Processing│─┤           │
│  │  • Kiosk Terminal           │   └──────────────┘ │           │
│  │  • Computer to Computer     │   ┌──────────────┐ │           │
│  │                             │──▶│  Filtering   │─┘           │
│  └─────────────────────────────┘   └──────────────┘             │
└─────────────────────────────────────────────────────────────────┘
```

Under conventional arrangements, salespeople, policyholders, and others request service by telephone, fax messages, and electronic mail. They might need information on the status of a payment or claim, might want a copy of an application or motor vehicle report, or might need many other pieces of information. In responding, a person checks the files; requests microfilm printouts; accesses the mainframe or local network; and provides the information by telephone, electronic mail, fax, or overnight mail. As the organization's customer base grows, more support staff members are needed to provide service.

In the future, a typical automated service facility will reside on a server within a local area network. When someone telephones and enters the proper identification and request number on the phone's touch-tone key pad, the automated service facility will connect to the mainframe, image processing system, and other databases on the local area network. After obtaining the necessary information, expanding data codes into English, and completing the necessary calculations and other processing, the system will fax or mail reports and any required images to the caller or use speech voice synthesis to answer the caller's questions over the telephone.

The Mobile Loss Control Representative

Loss control representatives perform on-site surveys of premises and activities to evaluate loss exposures. As the "eyes and ears" of the underwriter, a loss control representative does the following:

- Provides recommendations or remedial advice to insureds
- Develops an overall opinion of the risk based on the findings, conclusions, and recommendations of the survey of premises and activities covered
- Writes loss control survey reports
- Revisits the site to ensure compliance with previous recommendations

Loss control requires much expertise. Workers compensation insurance focuses on the safety of workers, while commercial property insurance focuses on the potential loss to buildings and contents caused by a covered event. Safety issues faced in a machine shop will be very different from those in a hospital. Loss control representatives must report large amounts of information for underwriting purposes. In addition, they must provide their managers with inspection reports.

How can the technologies discussed earlier in this chapter be used to automate the loss control function? Using pen-based computers instead of the traditional paper forms and notes allows the loss control representative to record information directly into an electronic device. Knowledge-based system applications, loaded on the pen-based computer, prompt the loss control representative for all information required to evaluate potential loss control exposures based on the insurance coverage provided, the type of business, and the different job functions performed at each of the locations. Once all of the information has been gathered, a draft of the survey report is constructed from conclusions and recommendations suggested by the knowledge-based system and information about the business downloaded earlier as part of the loss control work order. To complete the draft report, a neural net application can analyze all the information collected and evaluate the risk. As soon as the final editing of the report is completed or at the end of the day, the report can be uploaded to the insurer's underwriters. If a report is required immediately and the loss control representative has a cellular phone, the report can be transmitted from the car while the loss control representative is on the way to the next assignment.

Summary

New information systems technology provides insurance organizations with the opportunity to create an electronic workplace that will help them continue to improve service levels, increase information availability and accuracy, improve worker productivity, reduce the turnaround time of insurance transactions, and reduce administrative expenses.

Processing time can be significantly reduced by using electronic processes. Agencies and brokerages can capture new applications, loss notices, endorsements, and other transactions on a computer and can use EDI standards in sending them to insurance companies. Regardless of the level of automation an organization eventually achieves, some information will continue to be received on paper, and some of it through fax transmission. Papers or faxes can be entered directly in an image system and converted to electronic form. Once information is stored electronically, the insurer's information system can ascertain what types of transactions it has received, can analyze them through its knowledge-based and neural network applications, and can route those transactions to employee workstations for processing.

Information systems staff members are using new software development techniques and tools to provide new computer programs to users in development cycles that are shorter than was possible in the past. Knowledge-based systems applications are being developed to assist underwriters, claim adjusters, risk managers, and others in their jobs. Neural networks use parallel processing machines to recognize and identify callers from their voices for voice response systems and to recognize the handwritten characters entered on the tablets of pen-based computers.

The pen-based computer, mouse, and voice response systems provide users with new ways to interact with computers. Multimedia technology allows users to capture and display data in a number of new ways, such as voice, full-motion video, electronic photography, and electronic forms. Client/server technology combines the connectivity of networks, the flexibility of intelligent workstations, and the functionality of new software applications to locate computing processing at the best place for each transaction—at the employee's workstation or on a database server connected to a local area network. Workstation software makes interacting with information systems easier for users. Sources of software productivity improvements include object-oriented programming, network operating systems, and relational database management systems.

Databases give the organization's staff easy access to accurate data that can quickly be turned into useful information. When all users access the same data, duplications are eliminated, and errors are significantly reduced. Improved information access allows organizations to modify their work processes so that employees can complete most transactions electronically.

One of the challenges all organizations face when evaluating newer technologies is that those technologies often tend to be poorly defined. Rather than quickly decide what a technology can or cannot do, organizations should evaluate each new technological development to determine what it can do for their businesses.

Chapter Notes

1. Christine B. Tayntor, "The Next Frontier," *Systems Development*, March 1992, pp. 1-5.
2. Bijoy Bordoloi and Mary Helen Fagan, "Piloting Pen-Based Computers," *Information Systems Management*, Spring 1993, pp. 20-30.

Chapter 3

Managing Automated Activities

This chapter examines information resources management. Systems, networks, and information must be actively managed if information resources are to achieve the potential suggested in Chapters 1 and 2. An insurance organization's information needs are highly complex and evolutionary. They are influenced by changes in products, customer needs, market opportunities, capital markets, regulatory requirements, and many other forces. The relentless rush of new technology adds further complexity to managing information resources. Constant management attention is required if information systems are to produce and convey the information that organization members need to accomplish their goals. Moreover, top executives must be involved in managing information resources if the organization is to integrate the development of information resources with the development of organizational strategy.

Special Challenges in Managing Information Resources

Does managing information resources require methods or techniques different from managing other resources? To some degree, sound management practices do not differ. Nonetheless, managers typically concentrate on the particular area's unique challenges. These challenges in managing information resources include the following:

- Focusing on results rather than on technology
- Controlling expenditures
- Managing system-related change
- Fostering collaboration between users and information resource professionals

Focusing on Results

Automation technology is constantly changing, and new hardware and software often are dramatic improvements of existing versions. The danger to an organization is that concentrating on technological innovations might divert attention from the results that information technology should produce. The discussion that follows provides a series of distinctions in terminology that should enable managers to focus attention on results rather than on information technology.

Information Systems Versus Information

Automation developments receive the attention of many members of an organization. Staff members read about new hardware and software in newspapers, news magazines, and business publications. Employees see their workplaces and departments changed when new computer equipment is installed. If they have PCs at home, employees might be keenly interested in the latest hardware and software installed in the office and might consider buying the same items for use at home. Understandably, such staff members are likely to focus on the system's hardware and software rather than on the information that can be gained by using the system.

The first major challenge in managing information resources is to focus staff member attention on the information rather than on the system. Managers can do this by emphasizing the organization's objectives and the information needed to attain those objectives. Managers should periodically ask staff members to evaluate the information produced and to identify the items of information that would enable them to achieve their goals more efficiently.

Having Information Versus Achieving Results Through Information

Focusing attention on information is a means toward the goal of achieving better results through information. Although establishing specific goals for improving information might be desirable, such goals should be associated with higher-level goals expressed as the results of using information. For example, the goal of better customer information is a means toward the higher goals of improved customer service and increased sales to existing customers.

Managers can focus attention on results by asking questions of themselves, staff members, and other managers. When system improvements are proposed, managers should ask how the information will be used. Also, managers should periodically ask staff members, "What else could we accomplish if we had better information?"

System Performance Versus System Effectiveness

The distinction between system performance and system effectiveness also helps to focus on results. **System performance** refers to the processing efficiency of an automated system. System performance is measured by such criteria as processing time, waiting time, and downtime. **System effectiveness** refers to an automated system's ability to meet the needs of the organization. Thus, system effectiveness is another expression of the concept of achieving results through information. System effectiveness is judged in terms of user requirements. For example, a claims system is effective if adjusters can quickly obtain the policyholder information they need. A management information system (MIS) is effective if it produces reports that direct the manager's attention to problems. An MIS is ineffective if information that identifies problems is buried in pages of data.

Managers should not ignore evidence of poor system performance. System performance problems must be corrected before system effectiveness can be maximized. Managers should also direct attention to system effectiveness whenever systems are evaluated and changes are considered. Most important, managers should establish criteria of system effectiveness for their departments and units. Examples of measures that reflect system effectiveness are the average processing time for specific transactions and the rate of data input errors. Moreover, staff member complaints about a system reflect system ineffectiveness.

System Effectiveness Versus Organizational Effectiveness

Just as system effectiveness is a better yardstick than is system performance, organizational effectiveness is a better measure of end results than is system effectiveness. "Organizational effectiveness" refers to attaining the organization's goals on an ongoing basis. The organizational goals considered when assessing information resources should be goals that employees can link to the use of information. For example, profit is influenced by many factors besides information resources and would not be accepted as a direct measure of success in using information. In contrast, customer retention rates and average revenue per customer are measures of organizational effectiveness that link more directly to the organization's use of information.

Controlling System Expenditures

Controlling system expenditures is the second major management challenge related to information resources. A large insurance organization might have millions of dollars invested in equipment, software, and trained employees. Similarly, an insurance agency might have a major investment in personal computers, network facilities, and its main system, usually called the "agency management system," which this chapter will discuss later. In both cases, considerable sums are invested in tangible system assets, software, and in employee skills. Those assets are subject to rapid obsolescence as new hardware and software become available. Managers must periodically evaluate system and organizational effectiveness, determine directions for further development, and decide on expenditures for improving information resources.

Cost-Benefit Analysis

Cost-benefit analysis is a common method to evaluate an automation project or other investment opportunity. Cost-benefit analysis compares all of the costs associated with an investment against the value of the benefits expected from that investment.

Proposed automation projects compete against one another for funds that have been allocated to information resources. In addition, automation proposals compete against non-automation proposals for the organization's funds. Organizations seldom have enough money to invest in all of the opportunities that seem promising. Instead, difficult choices must be made. Organizational and departmental steering committees must choose or recommend the best, most cost-effective automation proposals for their organization. Despite its limitations, cost-benefit analysis provides a common framework for evaluating investment proposals, including proposals that have highly dissimilar benefits.

Measuring Costs

Some of the costs of a proposed automation project are known precisely. Examples are hardware, software, and installation costs. Other costs might be known to exist but are difficult to measure accurately. Examples include the cost of data conversion, the cost of lost productivity while learning a new system, and the cost of the time that information services staff members spend on tasks created by the project. Other costs might be difficult to identify. Examples include the cost of added security provisions and the cost of supervisory and management time associated with a project. Sound cost-benefit analysis must combine the less-certain costs with those that are known with greater certainty.

Estimating Benefits

Many of the benefits of an automation project seem difficult to quantify. What is the dollar value of faster service? How much is improved customer profiling worth to an agency? How much money is saved by a system improvement that reduces the frequency of errors in processing a type of transaction? Such benefits are extremely difficult to measure, and estimates are often necessary for cost-benefit analysis.

Estimates of the value of many system benefits might be subjective, but that does not mean that they have little validity. Decision scientists believe that managers can make meaningful estimates even though they might be unable to explain how they derived the estimates. For example, an agency manager might be able to say that "improved customer profiling is worth $6,000 to the agency," or, "I would gladly pay $6,000 for a system that gave us good customer profiling." Similarly, an insurance company executive might believe that faster service on quotations could allow the company to sell 5,000 more policies per year and that those additional policies would be worth $100 each to the insurer. As subjective as they seem, such estimates can improve cost-benefit analysis.

Cost-benefit analysis usually considers the timing of expenditures and benefits. All outlays, revenues, and cost savings that will occur in the future are converted to present dollars to accurately determine the value of an investment alternative. The procedures for adjusting for the timing of outlays and earnings are described in finance texts and in CPCU 8.

Qualitative Considerations in Purchase Decisions

Qualitative considerations are usually combined with cost-benefit analysis in making automation and other capital investment decisions. The qualitative considerations discussed here are particularly relevant to automation projects.

Meeting Reporting Requirements

Insurers must comply with the reporting requirements of regulatory agencies, statistical agents, and rate advisory services. Some automation projects are necessary to meet the requirements of the organizations to which insurers provide data.

Integrating Information with Organizational Strategy

Developing information resources is a major component of organizational strategy in an information-intensive business such as an insurance company, brokerage, or agency. For those organizations, the development of information resources should be integrated with strategic planning, as discussed in Chapter 1.

Some automation projects are selected because they are essential to the achievement of one or more strategic objectives. Conversely, automation projects might be rejected because they do not help the organization to attain strategic goals. Agency/company interface illustrates that information resources are linked to organizational strategy in insurance companies that distribute their products through the independent agency system. Insurance companies risk losing business volume and perhaps representation by highly automated agencies if the insurers allow their interface services to become inadequate or outmoded relative to the agency/company interface offered by competitors. Insurers cannot develop the business they want without adequate interface capabilities.

Maintaining Reputation

The need to maintain the organization's reputation or image is another qualitative consideration in automation investment decisions. Not all insurance organizations should be automation pioneers or develop state-of-the-art information resources. For many insurers and agencies, a sound strategy is to be a "close follower" of the pioneers and thus to avoid the risks and expenses of being an innovator. However, few insurance organizations can prosper with a reputation for having an inadequate or seriously outdated information system. For example, insurance agencies might lose business if customers doubt they have the information resources to match the service provided by other agencies.

Meeting Employee Needs

Another qualitative justification for automation projects is the value of meeting employee needs and requests. Employees could express strong preferences for systems that are easy to learn and use. Employees want systems that make use of their computer skills. They might suggest purchasing new workstations or printers because they have heard of their features or advantages.

Employee standards and expectations tend to rise as technology improves. Thus, employees could be dissatisfied today by system response times that were once considered adequate. Because an increasing proportion of insurance employees spend most of their time at computer workstations, their computer needs and preferences should be given great weight in evaluating system proposals.

Timing—Buying Now Versus Later

New hardware and software constitute a steady stream of better products into the automation marketplace. The price for a given amount of computing power tends to decrease over time. Consequently, managers who are evaluating systems might be tempted to wait for the next product to arrive. They might believe that breakthrough products would render today's hardware and software obsolescent overnight. They might remember dramatic improvements that occurred early in the history of computers.

Waiting for improved products is seldom justified. Technological improvements now generally occur not as giant leaps but as a series of steady steps. New versions rarely make existing hardware and software worthless. Instead, organizations can often incorporate the latest improvements into their existing systems by purchasing system upgrades and enhancements.

Automation users should carefully evaluate announcements of new products because features might be overstated, availability might be later than promised, and early users might find that some flaws ("bugs") have not been discovered or eliminated. For all of those reasons, delaying a properly justified automation purchase on the grounds that a better product will soon be developed is usually unwise. Rather than think of system improvements as dramatic innovations that last forever, automation users should view improvements as steps in a constant evolutionary process.

Managing System-Related Change

Another major management challenge related to information resources is the need to manage the many changes resulting from automation projects. Managers must be sensitive to the ripple effects as well as to the direct effects of automation projects. Ripple effects include changes in job procedures and employee roles, adjustments to inter-organizational information flows, and changes in staff training needs.

Managing Automation Projects

Automation specialists and users do much of the work of automation projects. Nonetheless, projects require close attention of the line managers of the departments and units involved. Managers and supervisors contribute to needs analysis, make suggestions for system design, authorize employee participation in projects, adjust workloads and schedules to allow participation in projects, evaluate and approve recommendations, implement new procedures, and evaluate project success.

The steps in an automation project will soon be described in this chapter. Managers must monitor project activities to ensure that steps have not been overlooked. Since a large project can involve several departments or units, many managers might share in the management decisions and duties associated with the project.

Managing Job and Role Changes

Automation projects usually modify work flows, jobs, tasks, and procedures. These direct changes are designed as part of the project, and their implementation is included in the project schedule. Other, less direct changes also occur as a result of automation projects. For example, a system installed in one unit might cause slight changes in how tasks are performed in the units that supply or receive its work.

System changes can affect informal groups within the organization. Having the latest equipment or access to sensitive information might raise some employees' informal status. A new system might result in relocation of desks, files, printers, and other equipment. Changes in the office layout might alter opportunities for interpersonal contact and lead to changes in social relationships among employees.

Resistance to change is a phenomenon familiar to most managers and can occur at any step in an automation project. Managers and employees can exhibit resistance to change. Even persons who welcome system improvements can show subtle signs of resistance as they confront changes in their jobs. Managers should watch for signs of change in the informal organization and use organizational development and other methods in responding to problems that might result.

Expanding Boundaries: Inter-Organizational Information Flows

Insurance organizations exchange increasing amounts of information with other organizations through electronic means. Agency/company interface and electronic submission of data to statistical agents and rate advisory organizations are two of the inter-organizational data flows that are now routine in the insurance business. Rapid progress in implementing electronic data interchange (EDI) standards has increased the ease of direct electronic communication with other organizations.

Information systems must evolve to provide data exchange with insureds, agencies, brokers, statistical agents, rate advisory services, regulatory agencies, financial organizations, service providers (such as hospitals, medical offices, and auto repair shops), insurance organizations, and other organizations. Insurance managers must ensure that staff members recognize the need to integrate their needs with requirements for expansive inter-organizational information flows.

Overseeing Training

Managers and supervisors are responsible for training their staff members, yet they might not personally design or deliver systems training. Instead, systems training might be provided by vendor representatives, information services staff members, or members of the organization's training department. Unit managers, supervisors, and team leaders are responsible for the results of training but might not have line authority over the trainers. Managers and supervisors have more direct control if system managers or experienced system users within the unit provide training.

Initial user training in connection with a new or replacement system is only a portion of what is usually necessary. Nonusers and members of other units might need familiarization training. Occasional users might require periodic refresher training. New employees might require initial training immediately after joining the unit. Employees who serve as backups for others require cross-training. In sum, training is a nearly constant and multifaceted activity that often involves trainers from outside of the unit.

Fostering Collaboration

Another challenge in managing information resources is to foster collaboration between users and members of the information services department. Successful system design requires extensive communication between and full understanding by users and system professionals. Collaboration is hindered by lack of knowledge about the other's field. Users and system professionals tend to use different languages. Insurance specialists tend to use the highly specific vocabulary of insurance coverages and procedures. IS department members tend to use the technical terms of the computer world. Opportunities for misunderstanding might be highest when users and technical experts know a little about each other's field and assume that all terms are mutually understood.

Users and system professionals might cite communication problems when new systems produce disappointing results. Users might believe that the system designers failed to communicate important details about how the system would operate. Systems professionals might believe that users failed to specify how they wanted the system to operate.

Managing Automation Projects

Organizations usually appoint project teams to automate manual tasks and to make major improvements in existing automated systems. The size and membership of a project team depends on the project's nature and scope. Users, supervisors, and managers might represent the using units on a project team. System analysts, programmers, user liaison representatives, supervisors, and managers might represent the IS department on project teams. The major steps of a typical automation project are as follows:

- Initiate the project.
- Conduct a needs analysis.
- Evaluate and acquire the system.
- Install the system.
- Train the users.
- Convert the system.

Initiate the Project

The first formal step in an automation project is a project request. Project requests could stem from an organization's system development plan, or they could result from problem recognition. The two major steps that occur during project initiation are a feasibility study and an initial budget estimate.

Problem Recognition

Many automation projects result from someone noticing or believing that a problem exists and requesting that a project be commissioned. The problem might be expressed in terms of system performance, such as processing delays or difficulty in using particular input screens. The problem might be defined in terms of system effectiveness. For example, a unit supervisor believes that error rates are excessive. The problem might be seen as one of organizational effectiveness. For instance, an agency manager might suspect that information deficiencies are to blame for the loss of several commercial accounts.

Not all problems can be solved by automation, and not all work flow problems have solutions that involve automation. Generally, automation offers a promising solution to a problem if the problem results from information that is inaccurate, poorly presented, or unavailable to those who need it when they need it. The manager of the department in which a problem is first recognized should ensure that the problem will be solved by information that is more accurate, more timely, or better presented.

System Development Plan

Some projects do not result from problem recognition. Instead, they are requested by the organization's steering committee or by department automation committees. These committees prepare a **system development plan** for the automated systems of the organization or department. A system development plan prescribes the actions that will be taken to expand and improve the information system. System development plans specify how systems will evolve to meet the strategic objectives of the organization or the long-term objectives of the department. A system development plan includes the new technology implementation plan described in Chapter 2.

Steering or department automation committees initiate requests for the projects needed to accomplish system development plans or to implement organizational strategy. For example, an insurer's decision to offer a new line of insurance or an agency's decision to add a new customer service might require one or more projects to upgrade the organization's information system.

Project Request

A **project request** is a formal request that a project be established. A project request should include a statement of the problem to be solved or the need to be met. The request should specify the following:

- Data to be included and excluded
- Processing to be performed
- Outputs of the new system
- Units that will use the system

Those specifications are starting points for investigating needs and developing systems to meet the needs.

Feasibility Study

The three purposes of a **feasibility study** are the following:

1. Defining system requirements
2. Determining the best way to develop the system
3. Conducting an initial evaluation of the costs and benefits of the new system

IS staff members rather than users are likely to be in charge of the feasibility study. They interview users, managers, and other IS staff members to evaluate the present system and to gather suggestions for improvements. They define the objectives to be achieved and the major features of the new system. They outline the major development options, such as enhancing the present system, developing a new system in-house, purchasing a new system, and purchasing software.

Initial Cost-Benefit Analysis

The feasibility study should try to answer the question, "How much will it cost?" The staff members who perform the feasibility study should perform an initial cost-benefit analysis. This analysis is clearly a preliminary one and will be revised, perhaps several times, as a result of the system design decisions that will be made later.

The feasibility study team prepares a report with its recommendations and requests executive approval for the project to proceed. As its name suggests, a feasibility study verifies the desirability of initiating an automation project rather than designing the system that might be needed.

Conduct a Needs Analysis

If a feasibility study results in approval for a project, a project team is formed. The team conducts a more detailed **needs analysis** than that done as part of the feasibility study. The project team uses the information it has obtained to solicit vendor proposals and to design the system.

Organize the Project Team

The executive who acts on the feasibility study recommendations should appoint a project team. The project team should consist of users and IS specialists as appropriate to each particular project. Supervisors and managers might be on the project team. The team leader might be an IS staff member or a member of the user department. The team's initial activities should be to plan the project and to establish milestones or activity completion dates to serve as control points during the project's life.

Gather and Evaluate Information

The project team gathers the information necessary to evaluate the present system and to specify the new system's requirements. Interviews are again conducted with users, supervisors, managers, and IS specialists. For a major project, the team might use the focus group method to probe participants' needs. The project team might repeat some of the work that was performed for the feasibility analysis, but the investigation is more detailed and thorough at this point. Months could have passed since the feasibility study, and the project objectives or scope could have been redefined as a result of the feasibility study and approval process.

The project team evaluates the information it has gathered and develops or revises specifications for the new system. The team might ask users to review the specifications and might revise the specifications to reflect user comments and suggestions.

Prepare a Request for Proposal

The project team prepares a **Request for Proposal (RFP)**, a document that conveys the desired system's specifications and asks vendors to prepare a proposal for the team's consideration. The RFP requires all vendors to thoroughly and consistently address system and project requirements. The project team is also likely to ask each vendor for a list of sites where the vendor's system can be observed.

The RFP serves as a safeguard to keep project team members from being distracted by the outstanding features of some systems as portrayed in sales literature and shown in demonstrations. If the organization develops automated systems in-house, an RFP is unnecessary. In that case, the project team should prepare a list of system and project requirements for the IS department.

Prepare a Preliminary Design

The project team evaluates the vendors' proposals and drafts a preliminary design or preliminary solution. This design specifies the preferred system's requirements and features. The preliminary design indicates the features that an organization wants even if purchasing an off-the-shelf system is likely.

Write a Design Brief

The preliminary design is included in the project team's report to management. The report, called a **design brief**, does the following:

- Describes the system to be developed or purchased
- Explains how the system meets the needs that have been identified
- Describes the project requirements and budget
- Serves as the basis for obtaining approval to proceed
- Provides information to support decisions within or about the project
- Facilitates communication among system specialists, users, vendors, and managers

Obtain Approval

After submitting the design brief, the project team might also make a presentation to executives. The size and complexity of the project usually determines the method of presentation. The executive(s) who authorized the project will decide on further action. The decisions usually take one of three forms: disapproval, approval, or approval with modifications. Once approval has been obtained, the team proceeds with the project.

Evaluate and Acquire the System

The project team should separately evaluate systems and the vendors offering them. Also, the team should seek and carefully evaluate references from a vendor's customers. As the team proceeds, it usually tries to reduce the number of systems for final consideration. Once the system is chosen, vendor negotiations occur.

Evaluate Vendors

Automation vendors range from small single-product firms to huge global organizations. A system purchaser usually depends on the vendor for service and system improvements long after a system is installed. For that reason, in addition to evaluating vendor systems, the project team should evaluate the following aspects of the vendors themselves:

- Financial stability
- Maturity of product line
- Vendor staff
- User group existence and activities

The financial stability of a vendor should be evaluated by reviewing the length of time the vendor has been in business, its profitability, and its financial resources. Ownership by a parent company might shed light on financial resources and corporate strategies.

Maturity of the product line is a second dimension for evaluating a vendor. Does the vendor offer a full product line? Have the products been tested through use in a variety of organizations? How technologically sophisticated is the product under consideration? Does the vendor have a record of successfully introducing sophisticated products?

The project team should assess the expertise and availability of the vendor's staff by asking the following questions: Are the staff members experienced in the technologies to be used and in the customer's line of business? Which vendor staff members will be assigned for system design, installation planning, installation, and testing? Who will provide service after the system is accepted by the customer? Will these individuals work effectively with the customer staff members who will install or use the system? Will the vendor's staff be available when needed by the customer? Will the vendor be able to deliver the system on time?

The project team should also evaluate the vendor's ability to provide support. What maintenance service is available? When service is requested, what response time can be expected? Is on-line troubleshooting available?

The existence and activities of a user group should be determined when evaluating a vendor. User groups provide a means for a vendor's customers to exchange suggestions for system use and to influence the vendor's product development efforts. User groups typically have regional and national meetings and publish newsletters and electronic bulletin board notices containing operating tips and other items of interest to system users. A user group that is financially and operationally independent of the vendor is usually considered preferable to one that is controlled by the vendor. If contacted, the user group staff or members might be able to provide information about matters such as the vendor's reputation for service and system improvements.

Evaluate Systems

The project team should evaluate the functions and features of systems under consideration. Unless the project requires a custom system, the vendor should demonstrate the system and provide literature describing it. The project team should get answers to the following: What will the system do? What will it be unable to do? Can the system be expanded to handle increased activity and to provide new functions or features? Does the system employ innovative (and perhaps unproved) technology, "old" (and perhaps obsolescent) technology, or a technology between these extremes? What on-line help functions are included in the system? How difficult will it be for users to learn to use the system?

Evaluate References

The project team should ask each vendor to identify organizations that use the system under consideration. Since the vendor is likely to provide only satisfied customers as references, the team should look further for references. The team should select organizations that are similar to its own organization in product lines, scope of operations, and information needs. Depending on the project's size and complexity, the team should contact one or several organizations and gather information by telephone or site visits.

Select the System

The project team evaluates all of the information gathered and selects the system that best meets the organization's needs. It is unlikely that the team will find a system that perfectly meets all needs and meets budget constraints. The team will probably reach a final choice by considering the advantages and drawbacks of those systems that were not eliminated at earlier stages of evaluation. The project organization might have to obtain executive approval of its final choice.

Negotiate

The project team might request the help of the organization's legal and purchasing staffs when negotiating the purchase of a system. Items that might be negotiated include price, delivery dates, the vendor's installation responsibilities, the training to be provided by the vendor, and the timing of payments.

Purchase terms usually provide protection for the vendor's proprietary interests and limit the user's ability to make copies of software. When negotiations are completed, the organization buys the system.

Install the System

"Installation" refers to several activities in addition to the physical installment of hardware and software. The system manager and project team usually collaborate in developing an **implementation plan** that details the activities to be performed. The role of the project team then decreases as the system manager assumes responsibility for overseeing installation activities.

The implementation plan identifies the activities to be performed, the milestone dates on which they should be completed, and the person responsible for each activity. The implementation plan helps the organization to avoid misunderstandings about the respective responsibilities of the vendor, IS department, and users. Items included in the implementation plan can include the following:

- Site preparation
- Workstation preparation
- Forms and supplies
- Equipment setup
- System testing
- Removal of components being replaced
- Revision of procedures
- Training
- Conversion

Train Users

Automation projects can produce disappointing results and frustrated employees if training is neglected, poorly delivered, or improperly timed. Training should be planned well in advance. A written training plan is appropriate for all except the smallest automation projects. The training plan should establish clear training objectives for the employees to be trained, specify training methods, guide the selection of trainers, and specify methods for evaluating the effectiveness of the training.

Set Training Objectives

The system manager and unit supervisors should set training objectives for those who will receive training on the new system and new procedures and for those who need to know about the changes being introduced. Primary users of the system need initial training in its use. Those who will use the system occasionally or who will serve as backups for primary users need cross-training. Employees who supply work to or receive work from the department receiving the new system might need familiarization training. The system manager and supervisors should also set objectives for later training, including refresher training and new employees' training.

Select Training Methods

Training methods should be selected well in advance to ensure ample lead time for preparing training materials and arranging training facilities. Classroom training allows many people to be trained at once but requires computer equipment in the classroom. One-on-one training allows each person to learn at an individualized pace but requires more instructors than does classroom training. Videotape training or on-line training might be available if the new system is off-the-shelf.

The number of choices increases if the vendor offers training at its site or at the users' locations. The vendor might provide some training under its standard purchase agreement but is likely to charge for additional training. Training at the vendor's training facility usually has several advantages. The trainers are usually experts in the system and experienced as trainers. Vendor-site training allows employees to learn quickly because they are free from the interruptions and distractions of the office. On the other hand, training at the vendor's site could be expensive because of travel costs. Other drawbacks might be that artificial data are used instead of those of the organization. The trainers might not be familiar with the work of the users or their organization.

Select Trainers

The ideal trainer is an expert in the system, an experienced and talented instructor, and an expert in users' tasks. Such a trainer knows the culture of the using organization and is available when needed. Since this ideal is not always attainable, the system manager together with the unit managers might have to decide which training skills are most important for the project. They select trainers on the basis of the priorities they determine. Trainers could be members of the vendor's staff, the users' units, the IS staff, the organization's training staff, or outside organizations. If many users will be trained, the primary trainers could train several employees who will then train other employees.

Develop Training Materials

Training materials typically come from several sources, including the system manager, IS department members, unit supervisors, training department staff members, and vendor representatives. They prepare exercises, class handouts, reference materials, training software, test data, overhead transparencies, and other materials needed for training.

Conduct Training

Training should be scheduled to coincide with system installation. Some training might precede installation, but portions of the training program might require access to the new system. Training should include discussion of the new system's objectives and benefits. Training programs should allow ample time for practice on test data before the system is used with "live" data.

Convert the System

The conversion process includes preparing data as well as transferring them from the existing system to the new system. Determining conversion procedures requires selecting the type of conversion, the amount of information initially loaded into each file, and the method of converting files. Exhibit 3-1 summarizes the decisions that must be made in planning to convert from one system to another.

Determine the Conversion Type

The three types of conversion are automated, semi-automated, and manual.

Automated

In **automated conversion**, data are transferred directly from one electronic system to another. To win sales, many vendors offer automated conversion of data from competitors' systems and from their earlier systems. Automated conversion eliminates data preparation and the staff time needed to enter data into the new system. Automated conversion also allows the conversion to occur in the shortest possible time. Drawbacks to automated conversion are that erroneous data are transferred to the new system and that an error in the conversion program will result in errors throughout the new system.

Manual

As its name implies, **manual conversion** requires manual entry of all data going into the new system. The data are entered by keystroke or by scanning devices. Manual conversion is necessary when converting from nonautomated to automated systems. An advantage of manual conversion is that it encourages "cleaning up" data by correcting errors and removing outdated and unnecessary items.

Exhibit 3-1
Conversion Decisions

> Determine Conversion Types
>   Automated
>   Manual
>   Semi-automated
>
> Select a Manual Loading Option
>   Full information load
>   Skeleton information load
>
> Determine the Conversion Method
>   Pilot
>   Piecemeal
>   Plunge
>   Parallel
>
> Convert the Data
>
> Evaluate the Conversion Accuracy

Manual entry usually requires substantial staff time. The unit supervisor might hire temporary employees for data entry. Doing so allows staff members to devote full attention to their regular work and reduces the time required for conversion. A drawback to using temporary employees for data entry is that temporary employees might not be able to identify errors in the data. The alternative to hiring temporary employees could be extensive overtime work by staff members. Having regular employees perform manual data entry offers the advantage of having the work done by people who will use the results. They might be able to "clean up" the data.

Semi-automated

In **semi-automated conversion**, some of the data are converted electronically while the remainder are entered manually. For example, automated conversion might be available for customer name and address information, but profile information could require manual entry.

Select a Manual Loading Option

Data entry for manual conversion usually takes considerable time. Two loading options allow use of the new system before all data are entered.

Full Information Load Option

Under the full information load option, the full contents of a file are loaded when the file is entered into the system. The most frequently used files are loaded immediately. The remaining files are then loaded into the system gradually, either as transactions occur or according to a loading schedule.

Skeleton Information Load Option

Under the skeleton information load option, all files are loaded initially; however, a minimum amount of information is entered within each file. The data required for the system to operate are loaded. For a policy record, the policy number, name of the insured, and expiration date might be required, but coverage information might not be required. Under this loading option, the remaining data are usually entered when the next transaction occurs or, for a policy record, at the time of renewal.

Determine the Conversion Method

The loading options determine how much information is initially entered into a file. Selecting a conversion method to determine when the files will be loaded is necessary. The four conversion methods are as follows:

1. Pilot
2. Piecemeal
3. Plunge
4. Parallel

All of the methods except the piecemeal method can be used for manual, semi-automated, or automated conversion. The piecemeal method is typically used only for manual conversion.

Pilot Method

In the **pilot method**, one person or unit tests the system. All of the files are entered into the new system, and the pilot unit uses the new system for a specified period of time. The system manager reviews the results before allowing the system to "go live" elsewhere.

Piecemeal Method

In the **piecemeal method**, files are gradually loaded into the new system by all users. Two choices exist for implementing piecemeal conversion. In the first, a file is entered into the system when it first shows activity. In the second, the file is entered when a designated event, such as policy renewal, occurs.

Plunge Method

In the **plunge method**, all data are loaded into the system as quickly as possible before the system is used. Plunge loading might require temporary assistance and overtime for staff members.

Parallel Method

The **parallel method** is regarded as an alternative loading method but applies more immediately to the process of going live. In the parallel method, all transactions are entered into the old and new systems, and processing is performed on both. If they both provide the same results, the new system is considered to be performing properly. If they do not, the discrepancies serve as the basis for debugging the new system.

Convert the Data

Data are converted after the conversion type, the loading option (if data are being converted manually), and the conversion method are selected. The new system can then be used.

Evaluate Conversion Accuracy

The unit manager is responsible for the accuracy of system information. He or she is likely to enlist the system manager in verifying the completeness and accuracy of data conversion. The unit manager might ask employees to make a complete verification of all files or might designate some employees to verify files after conversion. As an alternative or additional procedure, the system manager and unit manager might spot-check files. Any errors found are corrected.

Managing System Growth

Completing a system project seldom means the beginning of a quiet period during which an automated system needs little management attention. Information resources are constantly evolving. A visit to the information services facility of one of the largest insurers once prompted a comment that "the system changes every week" because a week rarely went by without the addition of new hardware or the elimination of old equipment. Insurance agencies and other small organizations experience a similar, if less dramatic, stream of system updates, upgrades, and enhancements to their turnkey systems. Two major challenges in the ongoing management of automation are maintaining system performance and effectiveness and deciding when to improve or replace a system.

Maintaining System Performance and Effectiveness

Managers and information system professionals often report that information systems are not fully used. Systems are not used to their fullest extent for several reasons. Employees might not know about some of a system's capabilities, might have forgotten about them, or might not understand the benefits they provide. Users might resist some features because they seem difficult to use. Managers might not be aware of all system capabilities or might not understand how some capabilities can be used to improve tasks, work flows, or decisions.

Organizations use several techniques to monitor and improve system performance and system effectiveness. Users should record all abnormalities and failures on a system log, and the system manager should periodically analyze all of the malfunctions that have been logged. Scheduled automation meetings allow users to report and discuss problems and to suggest improvements. Managers and information professionals can perform post-implementation audits to evaluate the success of system projects, and they can conduct periodic audits of overall system performance.

User groups, industry groups, or consultants can provide statistical data that help in assessing system effectiveness. For example, an agency manager who wants to evaluate the effectiveness of commercial lines processing might obtain published averages of "commercial lines commissions per commercial lines customer service person" and "commercial lines customers per commercial lines customer service person." Such averages, constructed from data collected from many agencies, might reveal areas in which the agency's results are above or below industry norms. The agency manager must judge the role of the automated system in contributing to the agency's results.

Deciding To Improve or Replace a System

Probably every computer system will eventually be replaced. The suggestions given above for managing system performance and system effectiveness should delay but cannot eliminate the need to consider replacing the system with a new one or, alternatively, purchasing upgrades and enhancements. In all but the most stagnant organizations, systems must expand to handle new customers, products, and services; to comply with new data reporting requirements; and to add new features and functions. System vendors sell upgrades and enhancements that add features or processing capabilities to an existing system. Despite the purchase of these system improvements, most firms still confront the need to replace the present system with a new one. In rapidly growing organizations, system replacement decisions often focus on *when* rather than *whether* replacements should occur.

Reasons for Replacement

Organizations might exercise initiative and replace systems to achieve specific objectives. They might also replace systems because problems have occurred in using the existing system.

To Achieve Objectives

Organizations can upgrade or replace a system to solve problems or to achieve new objectives. For example, a system can be upgraded to reduce the time required to process specific transactions. A system might be purchased to test a new technology, perhaps under the new technology implementation plan mentioned in Chapter 2.

To Solve Performance Problems

In addition to replacing systems based on such positive initiatives, organizations could be forced to replace systems because of the following problems:

- The system cannot be maintained.
- The system becomes inadequate.
- The system becomes obsolescent.

A system could become difficult, costly, or impossible to maintain if parts and service are no longer readily available. The system vendor or hardware manufacturer might have gone out of business or discontinued support of a particular system.

An automated system can become inadequate when the amount of data increases and the system must perform additional functions. The symptoms of system inadequacy are the following:

- Response time increases.
- The system runs out of storage capacity.
- Additional functions or features cannot be added.

The two reasons just mentioned—the system can no longer be maintained or becomes inadequate—are compelling reasons to replace a system as soon as possible. Organizations also upgrade or replace systems because of obsolescence.

Obsolescence

Obsolescence refers to the decline in value that most capital assets undergo when more productive assets become available. Simply, a computer becomes obsolescent when a better computer enters the market. Equipment is obsolescent relative to other equipment and relative to specific organizational needs. For example, a hand-held calculator became obsolescent for many business purposes when spreadsheet software became available, yet the calculator is still ideal for some applications. Obsolescence can occur gradually, as when a system progressively loses its value as better systems appear, or suddenly, as when the desktop publishing technology introduced in the mid-1980s made some other composition methods obsolescent virtually overnight. Obsolescence takes two forms, technological and economic.

Technological obsolescence refers to a decline in a product's mechanical or physical performance. A computer system becomes obsolescent when a product that better performs its functions becomes available. To illustrate, assume that a printer could produce an average of 250 policies per hour for an insurance company. If a new printer could print 500 policies per hour, the company's existing printer would become technologically obsolescent. Technological obsolescence is measured in physical terms such as processing speed, storage capacity, and the number of cells in a spreadsheet.

Economic obsolescence refers to the relative decline in a product's economic value or utility when a superior product becomes available. This decline in economic value occurs because the new product can provide the same service at a lower cost or can provide superior service at the same cost as the present product. The work the product performs is the crux of economic obsolescence, which is measured by the dollar value of the task or service provided. In the illustration given above, technological obsolescence could be measured by printing speed, and economic obsolescence could be measured by the average cost of printing a policy.

Technologically obsolescent equipment is not necessarily economically inferior or obsolescent. Additional information is often needed to determine whether economic obsolescence has occurred. The cost of the new product, the resale value of the existing one, the interest cost of the funds to buy the new product, and the tax consequences of the replacement should be considered.

Economic obsolescence should govern the decision to replace automated systems. In other words, computer systems should be upgraded or replaced not because better systems appear on the market but because the new systems reduce costs or increase the value of output.

One way to judge economic obsolescence is to estimate dollar values for technical benefits. For instance, assume that new software reduces by two minutes the average time needed to enter information on a homeowner's policy into a database. The value of the two-minute savings can be calculated by considering the average salary and benefit costs of the employees who enter the data. The value of the time saved is then used as the benefit factor in cost-benefit analysis to determine whether to purchase the software.

Agency/Company Interface

Insurance company computers exchange data with computers in rate advisory organizations, statistical agent organizations, motor vehicle bureaus, regulatory agencies, agencies, brokerages, and other organizations. Agencies and brokerages exchange data electronically with insurance companies, insureds, and other organizations. One type of this electronic communication—**agency/company interface**—is particularly important as a force that is changing how insurance meets the needs of its customers.

Achieving agency/company electronic interface became a goal of insurers and agencies once the capabilities of automation became clear. Agency/company electronic interface, known in insurance simply as **interface**, is seen as a critical factor in improving customer service and in reducing the cost of providing insurance. (Outside the insurance business, interface has the broader meaning of electronic data interchange between computers.)

The typical automated insurance agency has a main computer system known as an **agency management system (AMS)**. The AMS meets most of the agency's information needs in a fully integrated manner. That is, it maintains customer records, policy records, claim files, diaries, and accounting records and produces financial and management reports. The AMS could also interface with one or more of the companies represented by the agency. In addition to its AMS, some agencies have one or more special-purpose computers, such as a rating computer or a computer that interfaces with a particular insurer's computer system.

Interface Methods

The two major modes of agency/company interface are interactive and batch. Interface in either mode might use industry standards and might be achieved through an insurer's proprietary network or through an industry network. Generally, an increasing proportion of agency/company interface is single-entry multi-company interface (SEMCI), which will be described later in the chapter. Many of the interface concepts can be used in the direct-writing and exclusive agency distribution systems. SEMCI is an exception: it can be used only in the independent agency system.

Interactive Interface

In **interactive interface,** a person in the agency communicates with a company computer (and perhaps with a person in the company) by using a workstation computer or a special-purpose terminal. Interactive interface is a hands-on process in that someone in the agency operates a keyboard and reads a computer screen throughout the duration of the interface. Interactive interface can occur with only one company at a time. Telephone costs for interactive interface are high because of the time needed for the agency employee to enter data and respond to screen prompts.

Interactive interface uses company-provided screens, codes, and procedures and applies company-provided edits as the data are entered. If erroneous data are entered (for example, a four-digit zip code), an error message appears on the screen, and the mistake must be corrected before data entry can continue.

Batch Interface

In **batch interface,** agency data are collected, stored, and forwarded to one or more companies. Similarly, within a company many messages can be stored and combined into a single transmission for forwarding to an agency. Batch interface is not hands-on interface in that it usually occurs without the immediate involvement of people. Batch interface often occurs at night to take advantage of lower telephone rates. In a typical batch interface arrangement, one computer telephones another after business hours, and each then delivers the day's accumulation of messages to the other. Compared to interactive interface, telephone expenses for batch interface are low since computers exchange data at high speeds.

Batch interface lacks the on-line editing feature of interactive interface. When errors are detected by the computer receiving batch data, it creates error messages and transmits them to the sending computer, perhaps as part of the next night's batch transmission.

Standards-Based Interface

Standards-based interface in agency/company interface refers to technical specifications for the way data are formatted or expressed and the way data are transmitted electronically from one device to another. To illustrate, the date January 3, 2004 could be written in several ways, including 1/3/04, 1-3-04, Jan. 1, 04, 3Jan04, and 03 Jan 04. A standard specifies the way in which the date must be stated. Another illustration of a standard is specification of the sequence of items appearing in a homeowners insurance application.

Within the property/liability insurance business, electronic communication standards are established by ACORD (Agency Company Organization for

Research and Development), a nonprofit membership organization. Its members include insurance agencies, insurance companies, and vendors of insurance automation systems. In effect, ACORD provides the framework through which the insurance business sets its own standards. In addition, ACORD participates in national and international electronic data interchange standards-setting efforts and provides educational and other services related to industry automation.

ACORD standards cover both batch and interactive interface. The major advantage of standards-based interface is that screens, formats, and other elements are the same for all organizations that adopt the standards. Using standards reduces the procedures and forms that employees must learn and thus decreases the likelihood of errors. Without standards, agency employees might have to learn, conceivably, eight different homeowners application forms if the agency represents eight insurers for homeowners insurance. With standards, the one form is easier to execute and can be submitted to several insurers for quotations.

Insurers also enjoy advantages when standards are in force. If standards apply, an insurer (or network serving the insurer) does not have to reformat messages to meet the unique requirements of each of the various agency computer systems.

Despite the mutual benefits of standard interface, not all agency/company interface is standards-based interface. Insurers and agencies must bear significant costs in converting from company-unique to standard interface.

Proprietary Interface

Some insurers have created their own networks for agency interface. This arrangement is known as **proprietary interface**. To keep telephone costs down, the agency computer typically reaches the insurer by telephoning a regional connection point called a **node** rather than the insurer's data center.

Proprietary interface has improved over time, can now be standards-based, and can involve the agency's AMS or a single-purpose device known as a "terminal." (Terminal interface is discussed below.) Direct-writing and exclusive agency insurers might find that proprietary interface is highly suitable for their needs.

Network Interface

In contrast to proprietary interface, **network interface** uses a data communications network designed for use by many companies and agencies. The most commonly used insurance network and the organization that operates it are both known as **IVANS,** as Chapter 2 mentioned. The acronym IVANS stands for **Insurance Value Added Network Services**. The term "value added" indicates that the network performs functions that make data more useful or more usable, in addition to serving as an electronic post office. Like proprietary interface, connection to IVANS is likely to occur via regional nodes.

IVANS' value-added services include storing and "bundling" messages. For example, in one day IVANS might receive messages addressed to one insurer from 200 agencies. IVANS gathers these messages and sends them as one transmission to that insurer. IVANS might reformat messages to meet the requirements of specific computers. IVANS can send copies of a message (for example, an insurance application) to several addressees. Because it purchases telecommunications services in enormous volumes, IVANS obtains telephone rates that are significantly lower than those available to most organizations. With thousands of organizations on the network, IVANS provides connection points (nodes) in many communities, enabling further savings in telephone costs.

Terminal Interface

The earliest agency/company interface systems used **terminal interface**, or interface through a "dedicated" device. Typically, the insurer placed a "dumb terminal" in the agency. A dumb terminal has a screen and keyboard to enter and receive data, but it does not have a computer's processing capabilities. Personal computers are now sometimes used as terminals. Whether a dumb terminal or a PC acting as a terminal, the agency device is a "dedicated" or single-purpose device that is not part of the agency's AMS.

Terminal interface provides efficient data exchange. Terminal interface is, however, unsatisfactory from an automated agency's point of view because duplicate data entry is required. Data must be entered once in the terminal for communication with the company and again in the AMS for the agency's records.

SEMCI Interface

Many of the improvements being made in agency/company interface are driven by the desire to achieve **single-entry multi-company interface (SEMCI)** within the independent agency system. The duplicate data entry required by company terminal interface lowers the efficiency of an insurance agency. Efficiency is further reduced by the need for agency employees to master the different screens and procedures unique to each company. SEMCI eliminates duplicate data entry.

Two conditions must exist for interface to qualify as SEMCI. First, the agency device used for interface must be the device used for policy data entry rather than a terminal or computer operating as a separate system. Second, an agency staff member must not need to reenter or re-prepare data for each company. With SEMCI, once an agency staff member enters data and identifies the intended recipients, automation, rather than an agency employee, performs additional processing to transmit the data or to receive responses.

SEMCI does not require using ACORD standards or communication through IVANS. SEMCI is defined in terms of results rather than methods.

Progress in Achieving Interface

The paramount benefit of agency/company interface is improved customer service. Providing high-quality customer service is a major objective of virtually all insurance organizations. Today, service excellence is a moving target: customers' expectations rise as service improves and as they see the benefits of automation in other areas of their lives. Consider, for example, the consumer who pays bills by telephone, checks stock prices or orders plane tickets through a home computer, and receives immediate product availability and shipment date information when ordering clothing by telephone. That consumer expects the same fast response when requesting a premium quotation, reporting a change in exposure, inquiring about a claim, and requesting other service from an insurance company or agency. Providing fast and accurate customer service requires instant access to up-to-date information, a process that often depends on agency/company interface.

Improvements in agency/company interface should continue in the future. The direct-writing and exclusive agency distribution systems have achieved considerable success in using interface to improve customer service and internal operations. The independent agency system has achieved some success and is continuing to expand its use of interface. Progress within the independent agency system often requires organizations to weigh their own organizational interests against common interests.

As an industry goal, SEMCI is not yet within easy reach. Current developments focus on achieving **download,** the company-to-agency portion of interface, on a batch basis. Batch download allows a company to load and update policy information in an agency's system. This updating encompasses transactions such as renewals, endorsements, new policies, and claims information. Download can accommodate the insurance transactions constituting the greatest volume of work in an agency: renewals and endorsements. SEMCI might be the ultimate goal, but many companies and agencies are focusing on expanding their use of interactive-up/batch download interface.

Obstacles

Several obstacles hinder the expansion of interface to include more parties, more products, and more features. These obstacles might vary by distribution system, yet the direct-writing, exclusive agency, and independent agency distribution systems all face issues of costs, cost allocation, conflicting objectives, and technological choices.

Cost

Agency/company interface bears a high price tag. Company and agency systems have evolved over many years. Components or entire systems might have been developed years before interface was attempted. Rewriting the programming for those legacy systems to allow them to interface can be extremely expensive. Considerable cost can be involved in rewriting programs to convert from proprietary interface to standards-based interface.

Cost Allocation

The three major parties involved in developing interface are the insurance company, the insurance agency, and, because reprogramming might be involved, the agency's system vendor. The cost of developing new interface capabilities must be divided among them. Once interface is established, the company and the agency must bear operating costs.

Allocating costs is difficult if interface changes the tasks performed by the agency and company. With interface, the agency performs more of the data entry function than it does without interface. Having interface might foster the transfer of some underwriting authority from the company to the agency.

Differing Objectives

Companies and agencies share several objectives in using interface, including improving customer service, attracting and retaining desirable business, operating efficiently, and improving the company-agency relationship. Their other objectives might differ to some degree. Agencies seek to increase sales, reduce response time, meet client expectations, follow similar procedures for all insurers, and avoid errors and omissions claims. Companies want to control their books of business, develop a desirable agency force, and exert some control over automation developments. In addition, some insurers require, on their applications, information that other companies do not require. If this is the case, then the insurer's need for unique information runs counter to the agency's goal of standardizing procedures for all companies.

Differing Technologies

Sending electronic messages to several computer systems requires processing by an intervening system that transforms the messages into the formats required by each of the receiving systems. Several technologies can be used to do this transforming. (The IVANS format conversion function does not do all of the transformation that SEMCI requires.) No one technological solution seems to be accepted throughout the property/liability insurance business as the standard. The absence of a common technology is an obstacle to interface expansion.

Those obstacles might slow the achievement of SEMCI but are not likely to prevent its eventual attainment. The improved efficiency promised by full electronic data interchange between insurers and agencies is so important as a mutual objective that continued progress is expected.

Protecting Information Assets

Information resources deserve careful protection. In a positive sense, information resources are competitive strengths that warrant safeguarding. On the negative side, disruption or loss of information can paralyze the operations of a department or company.

One of the management challenges involved in protecting information resources is making trade-offs between protection and convenience. Another challenge is the difficulty of making protection a high-priority concern when many staff members have had little direct experience with losses stemming from security breaches. A third challenge is the complexity of information security: tangible and intangible information assets require protection against a wide range of threats.

Threats

The major threats to tangible and intangible information assets are the following:

- Natural perils—fire, flood, earthquake, windstorm, lightning, animals, liquid, temperature extremes, and dust
- Power supply abnormalities—power surges and power drops
- People-related threats—errors, abuse, theft, sabotage, and other malicious actions

Information processing equipment is vulnerable to the same natural perils that affect other physical assets, such as fire and earthquake. In addition, some computer equipment can be harmed by conditions that do not harm most other assets. These conditions include power surges, power drops, dust, humidity, and temperature extremes.

The people who might threaten information resources include outsiders and insiders. Outsiders include competitors, criminals, protesters, terrorists, and hackers. A **hacker** is a person who gains unauthorized admittance to a system. Originally the term had a rather benign connotation, referring to amateurs interested in the mental challenge of breaking into protected systems. The term now includes those whose motivation is greed, power, or the desire to do damage. Hackers, criminals, and others might access a system via telecommunications equipment, or they might enter the premises for that purpose.

Protecting Tangible Information Assets

Tangible information assets include the following:

- Computers
- Input, storage, and output devices
- Telecommunications hardware
- Wiring
- Software media
- Computer rooms and buildings

Levels of Protection

The level of protection given tangible information assets is likely to differ according to their value and to the value of the information they contain. Mainframe systems are likely to be in secured rooms or buildings. Personal computers, laptop computers, printers, and other less expensive devices are likely to be less well protected. The need for ready access to such equipment makes security more difficult, and employees might regard some protective measures as nuisances. Security of small computers should not be neglected, particularly since in a LAN system they could contain the organization's most valuable information.

Hardware, wiring, and media usually receive the same protection given other physical assets. This protection might include protection against power problems, theft, fire, lightning, and other natural perils. Protective measures include building design, fire-resistant construction, fire extinguishing systems, and similar measures. Surge protectors and uninterruptible power supplies can provide protection against too much or too little electrical power.

Access Controls

Controlling physical access is a major element in providing protection for tangible information assets. Data centers and other concentrations of computer equipment are usually protected by guard service and entry control devices (including card readers and devices that "read" fingerprints, retinal patterns, and other personal attributes.)

Protection against theft can be provided by the access control methods previously cited and by antitheft devices attached to equipment. The variety of special computer antitheft devices includes cables, security plates, alarm systems, and equipment enclosures.

Protecting Intangible Information Assets

Intangible information assets include the information within the organization and software programs, especially those unique to the organization. The computer programs and information in an insurance organization, in hard copy and electronic form, are vital and confidential to that organization. Programs and information in electronic form can be stored in a variety of locations, devices, and media. At any location, the information can reside in a computer processor, in disk drives, and in storage media. With network systems, the information can be located in offices throughout the organization.

Backup Procedures

Perhaps the most important protective technique is creating **backup copies** of programs and information. Computers can lose data for many reasons, including power problems, program errors, deliberate and inadvertent erasures, and mechanical failures such as "head crashes" on hard disk drives.

A typical backup procedure involves copying the entire contents of a computer's data storage onto tape or disk or into another computer. An alternative procedure is to make frequent backup copies of files in current use and to backup the entire system periodically. The backup disks and tapes should be stored in another location.

Security Classifications

Many organizations classify information for security purposes. One classification scheme is as follows: (1) general information, (2) confidential information, and (3) top-secret information. Another classification scheme is as follows: (1) nonessential records, (2) useful records, (3) important records, and (4) vital records. Using such classification schemes matches the degree of protection to the value of the information.

Access Controls

Software programs that limit access to stored information are the major means for protecting intangible information assets. Users are typically required to enter their log-on names and passwords to gain access to data. For greater security, some systems require additional identification through a key, a personal identification number, or another method. **Access control software** authorizes each user to do one or more of the following: read, add to, change, or delete a file. A user's authority typically varies from file to file. For example, a claims examiner might be authorized to view but not to change coverage information in a policyholder's file. An executive could have the authority to view all top-secret files but might be authorized to alter only some of the documents they contain.

Additional measures protect information in networks. Software provides access controls known as "network logical controls." These controls prevent users from browsing through a system. Encryption makes messages unintelligible to unauthorized readers. Encryption protects against interception from transmission cables or microwave transmission. Special devices protect systems against electronic eavesdroppers who try to pick up the unavoidable signals that all computers emit over short distances.

Antivirus Measures

Antivirus software scans computers for the presence of known viruses and removes them or prevents them from going into effect. Viruses are deliberately introduced programs that interfere with an automated system's operation. Viruses operate by infecting other programs and are spread whenever those programs are loaded onto computers. A virus might wait for an event to trigger its attack on a system. For example, the Michelangelo virus was so named because it triggered on March 6, the birth date of the famed artist. Viruses can alter video displays, modify or erase data, and hide or rename files.

Information Security Plans

Organizations should establish plans for protecting information resources. Information security plans, approved by a senior executive, can guide managers and information services professionals as they make decisions that influence the security of information and equipment. Information security plans should include the following components:

- Information access and security policies
- Record protection policies
- Record retention and disposal practices
- Audits of system use
- Disaster plan
- Recovery plan
- Restoration plan

Disaster, Recovery, and Restoration Plans

Disaster plans prepare an organization for an information disaster's consequences. They should specify the procedures to be taken before and during a disaster that disrupts computer operations. A disaster plan could include the following:

- Backup storage facilities and procedures (hot or cold sites)
- Staff assignments during and following a disaster
- Recovery procedures
- Restoration procedures

Recovery procedures specify the actions to be taken to continue information processing after a disaster. The actions include retrieving data from backup storage facilities, activating temporary facilities, coordinating activities at the backup and disaster sites, and restoring communications. Facilities used as backup storage facilities could also serve as recovery facilities. For example, a large organization with several data centers could use them as backup and recovery facilities for one another. An organization could contract with a service firm that operates a "hotsite." A hotsite provides backup storage and recovery capabilities in climate-controlled, secured facilities.

Restoration procedures specify the actions to be taken to restore a computer facility to full operating condition after a disaster. The first step in restoration is usually a detailed review of the damage to determine whether to rebuild or replace the facility. Damaged hardware must be tested for possible reuse or replacement.

Restoration procedures rely on checklists of equipment and software and of facilities requirements. The equipment and software checklist should indicate all current equipment, software, and supplies. The list should also indicate obsolescent and inadequate items. Hardware and software are likely to be replaced by newer versions. The facilities checklist should detail requirements for space, power supply, climate control, access control, and security measures.

Risk Management Approach

Some organizations follow a **risk management approach** to protect information resources. "Risk management" has been defined as the organized treatment of loss exposures. Exposure to the consequences of information loss is not unlike exposures to other kinds of loss.

The risk management process involves five steps:

1. Identifying and analyzing loss exposures
2. Examining the feasibility of alternative risk management techniques
3. Selecting the best risk management technique(s)
4. Implementing the techniques
5. Monitoring the program

The risk management process is described in CPCU 1. The purpose here is not to detail the process but to suggest its usefulness as a framework for managing the risks of loss associated with information resources.

The first step, identifying and analyzing loss exposures, usually involves estimating the frequency (how often) and severity (how costly) of each exposure. For example, major losses to giant mainframe systems have very low frequency but exceedingly high severity. Mainframes are usually protected by secure buildings, guard service, access control, and other measures. In contrast, loss frequency might be higher for laptop and palmtop computers, but the severity per incident is low. Those small devices usually receive less stringent protection.

The second step, examining the feasibility of alternative risk management techniques, includes exposure avoidance, loss prevention, and loss reduction. It could be possible to avoid exposure to the loss of equipment by outsourcing or purchasing information processing from an outside organization. Loss prevention measures seek to lower the frequency of losses. Antitheft devices that fasten personal computers to desks are loss prevention devices. Backup procedures illustrate the loss reduction technique, which tries to lower the severity of losses that occur.

Risk management also includes decisions about retaining or transferring the financial consequences of loss. Insurance is available for many information resources loss exposures. A data processing equipment policy insures hardware components but usually excludes data. Coverage for data processing media indemnifies losses when the media are active and hold information. Extra expense insurance and business interruption insurance cover the financial consequences of the loss of information resources in some situations. Fidelity bonds and dishonesty insurance cover employee fraud and embezzlement through use of a computer system. Coverage for small computer systems is available to PC owners and owners of small businesses. The need to consider such relatively specialized coverages adds to the value of a framework such as risk management for handling loss exposures related to information resources. In turn, the management of losses is an important part of an organization's overall plan for protecting its information resources.

Summary

Information resources are vitally important to organizations and require active, constant management. Information resources pose particular challenges to managers, including the need for a focus on results rather than technology. Focusing on organizational effectiveness rather than system effectiveness helps managers to plan for system development and to control system expenditures. Cost-benefit analysis plays a major role in system decisions, but qualitative considerations might control some decisions.

Managers are challenged by the frequency and scope of system-related change. Information resources usually evolve through a succession of automation projects. Each project could trigger job and role changes and resistance to change. Organizations use several structures to aid in planning and managing the development of information resources. These structures include a steering committee, department automation committees, system managers, and project teams.

An automation project consists of several stages. At each stage, information services professionals collaborate with users to find or create technological answers to work flow problems. Projects can be initiated under a system development plan, or they can be triggered by the recognition of a problem. After a problem is recognized and further action is authorized, a project team conducts a needs analysis. The team presents the results in a design brief. After executive approval is obtained, the team evaluates systems and vendors. The team then develops its design for the system to be purchased or created. Once the design is final, the team plans and completes installation and training activities. Conversion from an existing system to a new system requires selecting the type of conversion, the manual loading option, and the conversion method.

After a new system is implemented, that system must be managed for maximum effectiveness, and its further growth must be controlled. Focusing on system effectiveness as well as system performance is helpful. System logs, automation meetings, and other methods aid in the daily management of systems. Decisions to expand or replace a system could be based on many reasons. However, economic obsolescence, rather than technological obsolescence, is the key.

The need for improved agency/company interface plays a major role in decisions to improve insurance information systems. Interface can be in interactive or batch modes. It might but need not be based on industry standards. It might use a proprietary network or a common industry network. Currently, organizations in the independent agency distribution system are focusing on developing batch download interface as a step toward the goal of SEMCI. The expansion of agency/company interface involves overcoming several obstacles and is an expensive undertaking.

Information resources must be protected against threats from natural perils, power supply problems, and people-related threats. Tangible information assets receive the protection afforded other physical assets plus additional protection tailored to the specific vulnerabilities of computer equipment. Access control plays a key role in protecting both tangible and intangible information assets. In addition, backup procedures are critically important in protecting against mechanical failures as well as security threats. Organizations should develop information security plans. Security plans include disaster plans, recovery plans, and restoration plans.

Index

A

Acceptable performance measures, 15
Access, data, 12
Access control software, 92
Access controls, intangible information assets, 92
 tangible information assets, 91
Accuracy, evaluate conversion, 79
Achieving user focus rather than technology focus, 16
ACORD (Agency-Company Organization for Research and Development), 50
Adaptive systems, 39
Advantages of distributed databases, 45
Advantages of storage and retrieval applications, 27
Agency/company interface, 83
 cost of, 88
 differing objectives in, 88
Agency-Company Organization for Research and Development (ACORD), 50
Agency management system (AMS), 83
AI (artificial intelligence), 37
AMS (agency management system), 83
Analysis, cost-benefit, 62
 initial, 69
 needs, conducting, 70
Analytical tools, 13
Antivirus measures, 92

Antivirus software, 92
Application development tools and techniques, 29
Applications, artificial intelligence, 37
 image, storage and retrieval, 27
 knowledge-based systems, 38
 new information technologies, 54
Approval, automation project, obtaining, 71
Artificial intelligence (AI), 37
Artificial intelligence applications, 37
Assets, information, protecting, 89
 threats to, 89
 intangible information, access controls for, 92
 protecting, 91
 tangible information, access controls for, 91
 levels of protection for, 90
 protecting, 90
Automated activities, managing, 59
Automated conversion, 76
Automated service facility, 54
Automation meetings, 18
Automation project, estimating benefits of, 63
 managing, 65, 67
 measuring costs of, 62
 obtaining approval for, 71

B

Backup copies, 91
Backup procedures, 91
Batch interface, 84
Benefits of client/server systems, 34
Benefits of EDI, 49
Benefits of knowledge-based systems, 39
Benefits of pen-based computers, 37
Business activity, globalization of, 9
Business alignments, 9
Business climate, changes to, 2
Business implications of image processing, 28
Business needs, integrating information resources with, 1
Buying now versus later, 64

C

Case-based reasoning, 37, 39
Challenges of client/server systems, 35
Challenges of image processing projects, 28
Challenges of pen-based computers, 37
Change, system-related, managing, 65
Changing business climate, 2
Classifications, security, 91
Client/server systems, 34
    benefits of, 34
    challenges of, 35
    components of, 35
Clients, 34
Closer relationship with suppliers and customers, 8
Code, 30
    reusable, 30
Collaboration, fostering, 67
Command and control management, 5
    decline of, 5
Committee, department automation, 17
    steering, 17
Common data dictionary, 51

Components, client/server systems, 35
    graphical user interface, 41
    image processing systems, 27
Computers, pen-based, 36
    benefits of, 37
    challenges of, 37
Conduct a needs analysis, 70
Conduct training, 76
Controlling system expenditures, 62
Conversion, accuracy, evaluating, 79
    automated, 76
    manual, 76
    semi-automated, 77
Conversion method, determining, 78
    parallel, 79
    piecemeal, 78
    pilot, 78
    plunge, 79
Conversion type, determining, 76
Convert the data, 79
Convert the system, 76
Coordinating at lower levels, 7
Copies, backup, 91
Core business, 5
Cost allocation, 88
Cost-benefit analysis, 62
    initial, 69
Cost-effectiveness, 20
Cost of agency/company interface, 88
Costs, measuring an automation project's, 62
Customer satisfaction, 3
Customers, closer relationship with suppliers and, 8

D

Data, converting, 79
Data access, 12
Data mining, 39
Database, 44
Database management system (DBMS), 44
Database technology, 44

Databases, distributed, 44
DBMS (database management system), 44
Deciding to improve or replace a system, 80
Decision making, improving, 14
Decision support systems, 46
Decline of command and control management, 5
Delivery, document, improving, 14
Department automation committee, 17
Design, preliminary, preparing, 71
Design brief, 71
  writing, 71
Determine the conversion method, 78
Determine the conversion type, 76
Develop training materials, 75
Developing inter-organizational information flows, 18
Dictionary, common data, 51
Differing objectives in agency/company interface, 88
Differing technologies, 89
Disaster, recovery, and restoration plans, 93
Disaster plans, 93
Distributed database issues, 45
Distributed databases, 44
  advantages of, 45
  management issues in, 45
Document delivery, improving, 14
Download, 87

E

Ease of use in systems, 42
Economic obsolescence, 82
EDI (electronic data interchange), 18, 48
  benefits of, 49
  elements of, 48
  insurance industry standards for, 50
EDI issues, 51
EDI software, 50

Effectiveness, maintaining a system's performance and, 80
EIS (executive information systems), 46
Electronic data interchange (EDI), 18, 48
Elements of EDI, 48
Emphasis on service, 4
Employee needs, meeting, 64
Empowering employees, 7
Empowerment, 7
Estimating benefits of an automation project, 63
Evaluate and acquire the system, 71
Evaluate conversion accuracy, 79
Evaluate references, 73
Evaluate systems, 73
Evaluate vendors, 72
Evaluation, information resources, 19
Executive information systems (EIS), 46
Executive and managerial support, 53
Expansion, interface, obstacles to, 88
Expenditures, controlling system, 62
Expert systems, 38

F

Feasibility study, 69
Focus on core business, 5
Focus on customer satisfaction, 3
Focusing on results, 60
Fostering collaboration, 67
Full information load option, 78

G

Gather and evaluate information, 70
Globalization of business activity, 9
Graphical user interface (GUI), 41
  components of, 41
Groupware, 40-41
Growth, managing system, 79
GUI (graphical user interface), 41

H

Hacker, 90
Hardware platforms, 32
Having information versus achieving results through information, 60

I

ICASE (integrated computer aided software engineering), 30
Image applications, storage and retrieval, 27
Image processing, 25
 business implications of, 28
Image processing projects, challenges of, 28
Image processing systems, 27
 components of, 27
Image processing technology, 26
Imaging, 26
Implementation plan, 74
 new technology and, 53
Implementing new technologies, 52
Improving decision making, 14
Improving document delivery, 14
Improving processing of work, 10
Improving product development, 12
Indexing workstations, 27
Industry standards for EDI, 50
Information, gather and evaluate, 70
 having, achieving results through information versus, 60
 integrating organizational strategy with, 63
Information assets, intangible, access controls for, 92
 protecting, 91
 protecting, 89
 tangible, access controls for, 91
 levels of protection for, 90
 protecting, 90
 threats to, 89
Information flows, inter-organizational, 66

 developing, 18
Information overkill, 16
Information resources, 1
 integrating business needs with, 1
 integrating strategic planning with, 22
 managing, special challenges in, 59
Information resources evaluation, 19
Information resources objectives, 10
Information retrieval, 46
Information security plans, 92
Information services, 11
Information systems, 11
Information systems versus information, 60
Information technologies, 25
Initial cost-benefit analysis, 69
Initiate the project, 68
Innovation, employees and, 8
Install the system, 74
Insurance value added network services (IVANS), 85-86
Intangible information assets, access controls for, 92
 protecting, 91
Integrated computer aided software engineering (ICASE), 30
Integrating information with organizational strategy, 63
Integrating information resources with business needs, 1
Integration with strategic planning, 22
Inter-organizational information flows, 66
 developing, 18
Interactive interface, 84
Interface, 48, 83
 agency/company, 83
 batch, 84
 interactive, 84
 network, 85
 progress in achieving, 87
 proprietary, 85
 SEMCI, 86
 standards-based, 84
 terminal, 86
Interface expansion, obstacles to, 88

Interface methods, 83
Interfaces, graphical user, 41
Issues in distributed databases, 45
IVANS (Insurance Value Added Network Services), 85-86

J

Job and role changes, managing, 66
Joint development teams, 29

K

KBS (knowledge-based systems), 38
Knowledge-based systems (KBS), 37-38
    applications of, 38
    benefits of, 39

L

LAN (local area network), 32
Levels of protection for tangible information assets, 90
Load option, full information, 78
    skeleton information, 78
Loading option, manual, selecting, 77
Local area network (LAN), 32
Local and wide area networks, 32
Loss control representative, mobile, 56

M

Maintaining reputation, 64
Maintaining system performance and effectiveness, 80
Management, command and control, 5
Management control, self-control as replacement for, 6
Management information systems (MIS), 46
Manager, system, 17
Managerial and executive support, 53

Managing automated activities, 59
Managing automation projects, 65, 67
Managing information resources, special challenges in, 59
Managing job and role changes, 66
Managing system growth, 79
Managing system-related change, 65
Manual conversion, 76
Manual loading option, selecting, 77
Materials, training, developing, 75
Measures, antivirus, 92
    performance, acceptable, 15
        objectives-based, 15
Measuring costs of an automation project, 62
Measuring performance, 15
Meeting employee needs, 64
Meeting reporting requirements, 63
Meetings, automation, 18
Methods, interface, 83
    training, selecting, 75
MIS (management information systems), 46
Mobile loss control representative, 56
Multimedia, 51

N

Needs analysis, conducting, 70
Negotiate system purchase, 73
Network, local area, 32
    wide area, 32
Network interface, 85
Network transmission source, 51
Networks, local and wide area, 32
    neural, 37, 39
Neural network software, 39
Neural networks, 37, 39
New information technologies, applications of, 54
    implementing, 52
New technology implementation plan, 53
Node, 85

O

Object, 31
Object-oriented programming, 31
Objectives, automation projects and, 20
    differing agency/company, 88
    information resources and, 10
    replacing system to achieve, 81
    system development and, 21
Objectives-based performance measures, 15
Obsolescence, 81
    economic, 82
    technological, 82
Obstacles to interface expansion, 88
Obtain approval for an automation project, 71
Organizational strategy, integrating information with, 63
Organize the project team, 70
Outsourcing, 9
Outsourcing products and services, 9
Overkill, information, 16
Overseeing training, 66

P

Parallel conversion method, 79
Parallel processing, 36
Parallel processors, 36
Pen-based computers, 36
    benefits of, 37
    challenges of, 37
Performance, maintaining a system's effectiveness and, 80
    measuring, 15
Performance measures, acceptable, 15
    objectives-based, 15
Performance problems, replacing system to solve, 81
Piecemeal conversion method, 78
Pilot conversion method, 78
Plan, implementation, 74
    new technology implementation, 53
    system development, 68
Plans, information security, 92
Platforms, hardware, 32
Plunge conversion method, 79
Prepare a preliminary design, 71
Prepare a request for proposal (RFP), 70
Problem recognition, 68
Problems, performance, replacing system to solve, 81
Procedures, backup, 91
Processing, image, 25
    parallel, 36
Processing of work, improving, 10
Processors, parallel, 36
Product development, 12
    improving, 12
Product information time, 13
Products, outsourcing of, 9
Programming, object-oriented, 31
Progress in achieving interface, 87
Project initiation, 68
Project objectives, 20
Project request, 69
Project team, organizing, 70
Project teams, 18
Proprietary interface, 85
Protecting information assets, 89
Protecting intangible information assets, 91
Protecting tangible information assets, 90
Prototyping, 29
Purchase, system, negotiating, 73
    timing of, 64
Purchase decisions, qualitative considerations in, 63

Q

Qualitative considerations in purchase decisions, 63

R

Rapid application development, 29
Reasoning, case-based, 37, 39
Reasons for system replacement, 81
Recovery procedures, 93
Re-engineering, 12
References, evaluating, 73
Replacement, system, reasons for, 81
Replacing management control with self-control, 6
Replacing system to achieve objectives, 81
Replacing system to solve performance problems, 81
Reporting requirements, meeting, 63
Reputation, maintaining, 64
Request for proposal (RFP), 70
   preparing, 70
Restoration procedures, 93
Results, focusing on, 60
Retrieval, information, 46
Reusable code, 30
RFP (request for proposal), 70
Risk management approach, 94

S

Scanners, 27
Security classifications, 91
Select a manual loading option, 77
Select the system, 73
Select trainers, 75
Select training methods, 75
Self-control, coordinating lower levels and, 7
   replacing management control with, 6
SEMCI (single-entry multi-company interface), 86
Semi-automated conversion, 77
Servers, 34
Service, emphasis on, 4
Service facility, automated, 54
Services, outsourcing of, 9
Set training objectives, 74
Single-entry multi-company interface (SEMCI), 86
Skeleton information load option, 78
Software, access control, 92
   antivirus, 92
   EDI, 50
   neural network, 39
Source, network transmission, 51
Special challenges in managing information resources, 59
Standards-based interface, 84
Steering committee, 17
Stimulating innovation, 8
Storage and retrieval applications, advantages of, 27
Storage and retrieval image applications, 27
Strategic planning, integrating information resources with, 22
Study, feasibility, 69
Suppliers, closer relationship with customers and, 8
System, achieving objectives by replacing, 81
   converting, 76
   database management, 44
   deciding to improve or replace, 80
   evaluating and acquiring, 71
   installing, 74
   maintaining performance and effectiveness of, 80
   selecting, 73
System development objectives, 21
System development plan, 68
System effectiveness, 61
System effectiveness versus organizational effectiveness, 61
System expenditures, controlling, 62
System growth, managing, 79
System manager, 17
System performance, 61
System performance versus system effectiveness, 60

System purchase, negotiating, 73
    timing of, 64
System-related change, managing, 65
System replacement, reasons for, 81
Systems, adaptive, 39
    client/server, 34
    decision support, 46
    ease of use in, 42
    evaluating, 73
    executive information, 46
    expert, 38
    image processing, 27
    knowledge-based, 37, 38
        applications of, 38
        benefits of, 39
    management information, 46
    user-friendly, 42
    voice response, 47

T

Tangible information assets, access controls for, 91
    levels of protection for, 90
    protecting, 90
Team, project, organizing, 70
Teams, joint development, 29
    project, 18
Techniques and tools for application development, 29
Technological obsolescence, 82
Technologies, differing, 88
    information, 25
    new, implementing, 52
    new information, applications of, 54
    voice and speech, 47
Technology, database, 44
    image processing, 26
    implementation plan for new, 53
    write once, read many (WORM), 27
Technology focus, user focus as replacement for, 16

Terminal interface, 86
Threats to information assets, 89
Time, product information, 13
Timing of system purchase, 64
Tools, analytical, 13
Tools and techniques for application development, 29
Train users, 74
Trainers, selecting, 75
Training, conducting, 76
    overseeing, 66
Training materials, developing, 75
Training methods, selecting, 75
Training objectives, setting, 74

U

User focus, replacing technology focus with, 16
User involvement, 21
User satisfaction, 21
User-friendly systems, 42
Users, training, 74

V

Vendors, evaluating, 72
Voice response systems, 47
Voice and speech technologies, 47

W

WAN (wide area network), 32
Work, improving processing of, 10
Workstations, indexing, 27
WORM (write once, read many) technology, 27
Write a design brief, 71
Write once, read many (WORM) technology, 27